RUSSELL CROWE

The Biography

RUSSELL CROWE

The Biography

MARTIN HOWDEN

JB
JOHN BLAKE

Published by John Blake Publishing Ltd,
3 Bramber Court, 2 Bramber Road,
London W14 9PB, England

www.johnblakepublishing.co.uk

First published in paperback in 2010

ISBN: 978 1 83458 265 6

British Library Cataloguing-in-Publication Data:

A catalogue record for this book is available from the British Library.

Design by www.envydesign.co.uk

Printed in Great Britain by CPI Bookmarque, Croydon, CR0 4TD

1 3 5 7 9 10 8 6 4 2

Papers used by John Blake Publishing are natural, recyclable products made from wood grown in sustainable forests. The manufacturing processes conform to the environmental regulations of the country of origin.

Every attempt has been made to contact the relevant copyright-holders, but some were unobtainable. We would be grateful if the appropriate people could contact us.

CONTENTS

PROLOGUE

It was 1994 and a young actor was auditioning for a role in a film that has since been acclaimed as one of the best movies of all time. Most actors aiming to make their mark in Hollywood would have sat nervously and waited patiently for their chance to impress. A nod in agreement here, a smile there and a polite shake of the hands at the end thanking them for their chance.

The intense young man sitting in front of the casting director was no such actor. Having explained in no uncertain terms that he should be given the part in *The Shawshank Redemption* above everyone else, despite his lack of Hollywood experience, he left the room confident that he had stated his case.

'The producer chased after me,' the actor recalled in a 2000 interview, 'and said: "You've got to get smart, kid. You can't just come into meetings and be that honest, because no one is going to care."'

He was then given the advice that he should put on an

American accent and do everything he could to convince them that he was from there.

'I told her that if I could con a director into giving me a role, I wouldn't want to work with him, because I'd believe he was fucking stupid. When I meet a director who understands what the job of acting is, then I'll work with him.'

Whether things actually happened the way he said it did is beside the point – it was an encounter that sums up Russell Crowe perfectly.

Straight talking, self-confident and possessing of an immediate dislike for anyone who doesn't take what he does seriously are qualities that have always been present in the actor. Of course, that also seems to go hand in hand with insecurity issues and a striving for acceptance and to be loved. But in a town where studio bosses like their films made with minimum of fuss, that sort of behaviour is flagged as one thing and one thing only – trouble.

Russell approaches his roles with an intensity that other actors can't – and won't – reach. And woe betide anyone who can't see that for themselves.

It's something that has always been with him – and it still rages inside now. Russell wants his roles to mean something, and even now he is dismissive of actors who have hit the big time and rested on their laurels.

'I don't use my "celebrity" to make a living. I don't do ads for suits in Spain like George Clooney, or cigarettes in Japan like Harrison Ford. And on one level, people go, "Well, more fool you, mate, because there's free money to be handed out." But to me it's kind of sacrilegious – it's a complete contradiction of the fucking social contract you have with your audience. I mean, Robert De Niro's advertising American Express.

'That kind of credibility thing doesn't get me any Brownie points at all. There doesn't seem to be that understanding of why you bother to not prostitute yourself.'

A quick look at his background and you would be excused for thinking that Russell was always destined for a life in films. His parents, Alex and Jocelyn Crowe, his grandfather and his mother's godfather were all involved in the movie world.

But his parent's involvement in the industry was limited to on-set catering, while his grandfather, Stan Wemyss, was a film documenter during World War II – a job that he did so well that he won an MBE for his bravery and was lauded by his peers for his stark, graphic black-and-white images of troops under fire.

That said, his family's involvement with the industry meant that it was a world that Russell could flit in and out of whenever he chose. 'From a very young age I spent the hours after school, weekends and holidays on film sets. I ran around knocking on all the doors and annoying the adults, you know? It took away that mystery. I knew when something came on television that there was nothing behind that façade.'

Growing up in this environment was no doubt thrilling for a young mind but, through observing what worked, what didn't and what different directors wanted, he was almost learning a new language. And it was a language that agreed with him, fitting in perfectly with a working environment that is far more intense than most.

Being an actor is not for everyone. It can be tedious, with hours upon hours spent waiting around and it can mean fits of rage because the pressures and long hours become common. But, it is all done to serve the script, and when you step up to utter your dialogue, everything that has gone before is forgotten in an instant. That magical moment when it's just you and your co-stars – nothing else matters. The arguments, the endless discussions about the script and the occasional stroppy moment that could get you fired in any other industry mean nothing if you can bring it together when it matters.

You could say that Russell fell into the job because of his childhood surroundings, but then you could just as easily say that Russell was always destined to flourish in these surroundings.

His blistering screen performances have made him one of the greatest actors of his generation. But his headline-grabbing antics off-camera have also ensured that he's become one of the most read about as well.

In short, he's a movie star in every sense of the word. A mongrel of Hollywood history – the glamour and stoicism from the early days of the film industry blended with the intense method acting of the 1960s and 1970s.

This is his story.

CHAPTER ONE

THE BEGINNING

'He was always the leader.'

– Jocelyn Crowe, his mother

Russell Ira Crowe was born on 7 April, 1964, much to the joy of his parents and the bemusement of his older brother Terry. He was born in Wellington, New Zealand – a city that would become synonymous with Hollywood fantasy epics such as *The Lord of the Rings* and the recent *King Kong* remake. But at that time Hollywood was just as otherworldly to Wellington as Middle Earth. It was sport that had a hold on Wellington and New Zealand – and Russell was born at a time when the country was still giddy from a triumphant win over the South African cricket team – thanks mainly to a dogged determination and plucky battling spirit that saw them triumph despite the odds being truly stacked against them.

There's a similarity to Russell's own battle in making it to Hollywood. As he said himself, 'Sure, luck is part of it.

But I believe you are the master of your own destiny. A lot of people go, "OK, I'm born in Wellington and I'm not supposed to go and make feature films in Hollywood. What are the chances of that? Pretty damn slim." They accept that and maybe I didn't accept that.'

Russell's was a close family, and while they didn't feast on the banquet of the movie industry, the crumbs that would fall down would be just enough to get by. Jocelyn and Alex's love for each other would be the foundations that Russell would rest against when things went bad, and he has chosen to build a similar foundation for himself with his wife Danielle. His parents were hard-working, full of generous spirit and old-fashioned values spliced with a bohemian and free-spirited attitude befitting of their nomadic life – moving from one place to another depending on their jobs.

Ray Martin, the Australian chat show host, said, 'Russell's very close to his parents and brother, Terry. He adores them. If you want to see him go berserk, just insult his mum and dad.'

Russell points at two deaths in his family that bonded them. 'My mother's sister [Raewyn] committed suicide when she was 21. Slashed her wrists in the bath. And my father's youngest brother [Charlie] died in a scuba-diving accident when he was 17. It just hadn't occurred to me what my father would have been able to say to my mother when she lost her sister, because he had had the same experience, and how close that must make them.'

His family wasn't religious in the slightest – and when it came to the decision of whether to christen, his mother said, 'Look, I was christened in the Church of England, and my stepfather forced me to go to a Catholic church. My husband was christened in the Church of England. But we think that our sons, when they're old enough, should make that decision themselves.'

Russell would go on to have an 'odd relationship' with religion – and actively sought out different religions to see which was the right one for him. 'Although I wasn't brought up in a religious household, I'm a very inquisitive person about it, and, just the same as with my acting, I've taken things from various sources that mean something to me.'

When he was four, he moved to Sydney, Australia after his grandfather convinced his son that he should stop working for a scaffolding company (as he was at that time) and open a stainless steel muffler shop in Australia – as Stan had the patent for stainless steel mufflers.

'And so my father sort of sold up everything and went and did that,' Russell added. 'Which didn't turn out to be a very good move, and my parents at that stage went into film catering.

Australia was a country that would play a major part in his life and it's where most people assume he was born. Several magazines and media outlets tag him as the 'Aussie actor' and he is closely linked to his adopted homeland.

Growing up around film sets sounds like a magical time for young children, especially ones with an unlimited imagination and a need to soak up everything around them like a sponge. At six, Russell got his first taste of being an actor when he appeared in an episode of the then-popular Australian wartime drama series *Spyforce*, which ran from 1971 to 1973. His parents were working on the show, and Jocelyn's godfather, Howard Rubie, was directing the 1972 episode *The Saviour: Part 2*.

The show, which starred Jack Thompson, was an adventure series revolving around the Australian Military Intelligence Operative in the South West Pacific during World War II.

Russell was asked to appear with a group of children for a scene. Maybe it was part nepotism, part driving need to stand out, or a bit of both, but Russell appeared smack right in the middle of the group and even got a speaking part.

His mother remarked that for years after his screen debut, dressing up and acting out was a large part of his life. So was his thirst for being front row and centre, no matter what he was doing.

Russell remembered that he would 'look at the 28-year-old guy playing the war veteran in a film and tell my parents: "I don't know why the director doesn't see me in that role. I might be a little short, but I can do it."'

It was a childhood full of untapped imaginations reined in only by what was being produced at that time in the studio. He ran through studio sets with wild abandon, gleefully opening himself up to whatever world the director had in mind.

'But I was never a child star,' he insists, 'I was a child extra. My parents were location caterers, so I was the annoying little kid on the set.'

He told *Interview* magazine in 2005, 'Mom and Dad were caterers, so there was always information about castings and stuff. And it just so happened that they were working on a TV set, so in order for us to spend time with our parents, we would be on the set and walk around locations and play with props, or see half a submarine built inside a building. You'd get a different perspective on the whole thing because you'd know that it was all manufactured. I was just very interested in it all.'

If he wasn't running around sets, he and the rest of his family would be watching TV at night. He recalls a routine that the family would adhere to religiously. 'My family used to be obsessed with *Dallas*. We used to all gather together on a Tuesday night and it would be the one night of the week we were allowed to eat on TV trays in the lounge ... The first couple of seasons of *Dallas* ... I was into that.'

Russell fully believed, as most youngsters do, that he was meant for something. And he knew it would be linked to performance. 'I used to have these very strange situations where I'd be walking down the street and I would imagine people calling out my name. I was as optimistic and as full of hope as anybody could be. Lots of things didn't turn out the way I wanted them to when I was a younger fella, but I didn't lose that thirst to understand what it is that I could do well.'

In another interview, however, he noted, 'I was shy. I was the sort of kid who would sign up for a talent quest and then, having done all the rehearsal and all the work, not turn up.'

When he wasn't around film sets, Russell would spend many an hour at the Wemyss family house, where his grandfather ran a little studio and film theatre. 'He and Stan were so alike, both artistic, both perfectionists,' his grandmother recalled. 'Now when I see Russell he's like my late husband when I first met him.'

His burning ambition was very much evident from a young age, as was a competitive attitude that still blazes inside him today. His grandmother remembers that he would throw his racquet onto the court if she ever beat him at tennis.

'He got really angry,' Joy recalled, 'threw a temper tantrum and chucked his racket down the length of the court. Eventually he calmed down and shook my hand, but he didn't like telling his parents that Granny had beaten him!'

The young Russell was only interested in performing – whether it was dressing up as a pirate, jumping off the ghost train near Sydney Harbour with his friends and terrifying the other passengers, or mimicking the actions and voices of family and friends. 'I was always an annoying little bastard and an embarrassment to my parents. I'd mimic their friends and my mum would say, "Don't worry about Russell, he's a bit mental."'

He briefly took an interest in writing. His morbid written work, which always had 'everyone dead by the end' intrigued one of his first school teachers – Elizabeth Morgan – who remembered him as a 'darling child, a lovely chubby little boy with those cheeks that you could push'.

Russell recalled, 'I'll always value what she did for me. She activated all the creative things inside me. Ms Morgan asked me to sing once. I sang *Ben* by Michael Jackson. She looked me in the eye and said: "That was a very special performance."'

Talking to the American writer James Lipton, he said, 'I would do these war plays, where basically everyone would just run around the stage and die, but there'd be some kind of point to it. Each week there'd be a new episode or whatever and I'd spend most of Wednesday and Thursday making uniforms out of paper which I would then pin to the costumes of the cast members.'

Russell was seen as a tough guy at school – as one childhood friend, who refused to be named, recalled to the *Sunday Times* in 2002, 'They were scared of him. He was one of the toughies – boisterous, loud, a show-off. But nice, not nasty.'

Despite a small role in *The Young Doctors* when he was 12 – 'I walked into a casting agent's office and said:

"Give me a gig." I was very practical' – performing held less and less interest for Russell as he matured – sports and music were preferred when he moved to Sydney Boys High School.

There he was remembered as an energetic and cheeky student. His schoolmate, Troy Sermon, said, 'He was always flamboyant. He had that drifty flair about him. He had a way of doing things, over-dramatising things a little bit.'

Another former pupil, Tony Hannon, added, 'He was an independent spirit, interested in everything. He spoke his mind, wouldn't put up with shit.'

Russell was the ringleader of a small group of mates – a 'rabbly type of mob' according to one of the gang, Blake Veverka. 'There were half a dozen of us,' he remembered. 'He'd go to Sydney Girls High, and try all kind of things to get their attention, make them laugh.'

It shouldn't be a surprise to see Russell looking elsewhere for success. His childhood was something of a nomadic life, moving here and there – flats above the hotels and bars that his parents managed after they left the catering business would be his temporary shelter. He and Terry would help out by changing kegs and Russell worked as a short order cook as a short-order cook.

'My dad was a pub manager. He didn't own a house until I left home, but he'd run pubs for other people,' said Russell. 'When there was a bit of a lull in that at one point, they started cooking in a garden bar for this guy who taught my dad a little bit about the pub game. Then in '72 a guy offered my dad his own pub to run, so for six years solid we lived in the pubs where my father worked. We didn't live in a house again until 1978.'

It was then, at 14, that Russell's world was turned upside down when his dad moved his family back to New Zealand to run a pub in Auckland.

The Potter's Wheel was a hotel. 'It's a tavern, really. It was part of a licensing trust in the west of Auckland. It was the job my father found in order to finance moving the family from Australia back to New Zealand. They used to serve beer in glass jugs roughly the size of a two-litre pitcher. And if a problem started in the room, they'd start throwing their jugs.'

It was a move that Russell didn't cope well with. Being part-Maori from his father's side, he struggled with his heritage when he was younger. His great uncle Huturangi Wemyss remembers, 'His mother asked me to have a talk to him about it one day. He was a teenager and he was disrespectful of the whole thing, so we sat down and had a chat. He was all right after that.'

Russell says now about his heritage, 'I've seen racism from both sides of the fence. My dad was a hotel manager for a while, back in New Zealand: the nickname for the hotel was The Flying Jug – this place was famous for fights. So I've seen racism from Maori to Samoan, Tongan to Maori, not just white to black. My maternal grandfather's mother was Maori. I have an option to vote on the Maori roll. And I've been bashed in New Zealand for being white. You can't stop and say, "Excuse me, my grandfather's mother was a Maori."'

After enjoying a fairly positive experience at Sydney Boys High School, his subsequent time at Auckland Grammar School was not so good. According to its website, the school helps boys to 'discover their individual strengths and weaknesses and affording them opportunities to feel good about themselves', but it seemed Russell found anything but that during his time there.

Not only did he hate having to wear the rigid school uniform – in this case roman sandals – but he found his creative talents stifled by the school's somewhat prioritised take on sporting prowess over academic endeavours. Even winning the class's English prize couldn't gloss over the feeling that his creative talents weren't being nurtured.

While sport was a huge hobby to Russell, it was never a realistic career option. In fact, the sporting tradition of his family would cast a shadow over Russell. 'Sure I had the potential to possibly play in an under-11 side but not really the ability or the desire and, besides, everyone else was bigger than I was,' he would say later.

Russell's cousins Martin and Jeff Crowe enjoyed something of a hero status at the school because of their cricketing abilities – their father was a renowned cricketer too – and they would go on to prove that at the top level. Not surprisingly, being dubbed the 'cousin of the cricketing Crowes' – or the 'singing cousin of the cricketing Crowes' when he began to experiment with music – was a tag that didn't sit well with the fiercely ambitious Russell.

Frustrated with school life, Russell and Terry were transferred to Mount Roskill Grammar. 'I wasn't expelled or anything but let's say it was a very amicable parting,' Russell said in an interview with New Zealand's *Woman's Weekly*.

Mount Roskill's former English teacher, Warren Seastrant, remembers of Russell: 'He was unhappy at Auckland Grammar, but he wasn't expelled. It was decided that he would go into my class because he had a little bit of form.'

The school's former deputy principal, Bob Laing, recalled, 'He had a few hassles there. He'd get his backside caned for various things he thought weren't fair. He wasn't rude to teachers, he wasn't bolshie – he just had a strong personality.'

While he now had more success in being creative, Russell was acting like most teenagers – disillusioned with what school offered and with no real path to follow.

'The hooded eyes and the cool disengagement,' remembered Seastrant. 'He had a great deal of self-assurance – superficial self-assurance at least. A lot of the prescribed arrogance was part of the image he was projecting. Yet he could switch it on. He was like a peacock on speed.

'He was good fun, basically a decent guy. He had a bit of a career of disruption. He would do enough to get by, usually at the C-Plus/B-Minus level. He was capable of much more.'

Russell's home life only added to the fiery discontent inside him. Fights and screaming arguments would be a regular occurrence because of his surroundings in a pub. 'When people drink they go to a lot of weird places emotionally,' he remembers. 'I've been in a room where 50 people are punching each other because they're drunk. I was basically a kid faced with adult fury. This is tattooed on my brain.'

Appalled by what he saw, Russell became more determined than ever to make something of himself – and not be someone who propped himself up on a barstool, with brawling as a pastime to break up their daily routine.

And it was music, not acting, that Russell first tackled in a bid to prove he was more than just a cousin to a couple of cricketers.

CHAPTER TWO

CROWE THE SINGER

'They all went rocketing straight to the bottom of the charts.'

– Russell Crowe

As a youngster, Russell would strum along to popular songs on the radio with a tennis bat, sweeping brush or his imagination doubling up as a guitar. At nine, he would write songs about 'love and all that sort of stuff'. His role model and inspiration? 'It's really fundamentally boring, but it was Elvis.'

Russell had been brought up immersed in the world of acting so he had also seen the hard work that went into achieving the results seen on TV or heard on radio – as well as the dogged efforts needed to make yourself seen or heard.

In the case of music, it was through the scores of live bands that would play at his parents' pubs. There he would see them trying their luck at entertaining the crowds, and he would be enthralled at how they used their audience to their advantage. One act in particular that he enjoyed watching was rock 'n' roll singer Tom Sharplin – and the young kid full of ambition bemused the musician. He returned the compliment by encouraging the teenager to try his hand at forming his own band.

Plucking his band members from his school, all with dreams of making it big as music superstars, was the easy part. How would The Profile stand out from the millions of kids who do it every day? Russell being Russell, he would do it the same way that he seemingly does everything – with an unwavering self-belief and refusal to make nice for the sake of it even if, in this case, the talents didn't quite match his expectations.

They would turn up at school talent shows, placing themselves in the front row and antagonistically turning their backs on other bands when they began performing.

Despite spending hours performing mod songs in either Russell's garage – which would normally see his dad pop his head round the door, offering words of encouragement – or in bandmate's Mark Staufer's house, they would soon split up. But unlike most school bands, where members leave the music behind and take on normal jobs content in the knowledge that at least they gave it a shot – Russell would persevere.

A fear of failure drives him as much as the need for success, and he was firmly aware that, with a brief excursion into punk with the band Dave Deceit and the Interrogatives aside, he was leaving school with a burning ambition to stand out but nothing as yet to show for it.

An insurance company was one of the first places that Russell found work, but it was merely something to tide him over as he tried to get his foot in the music industry door. Again, as with the acting world when he was a youngster, he got a break through connections.

Sharplin, who remembered offering advice to Russell when he had performed at his father's bar, was keen to help him. 'He didn't know the meaning of no,' he recalled. 'He'd constantly be asking advice, not just about the music, but the mechanics of show business.'

Sharplin's bass player, Raymond Eade, remembered, 'When I saw Russ, I thought "There's something about this guy." I thought he was obviously going to get somewhere. He used to come into the dressing-room and chat with us. He was a nice little kid, I thought. Then I found out he was very interested in the music and very interested in the show.'

Sharplin's club King Creole was where the 17-year-old Russell was ever-present – and where he would perform DJ duties as well as immerse himself in music and the tricks of performing on stage.

Despite revelling in his new surroundings as a DJ – a plum job for a teenager who was overjoyed at being the star of the show for a brief moment and reaping the rewards of female attention – it was clear to many that DJing was not going to be a long-term career for Russell.

'I don't think he particularly wanted to be a DJ,' Eade remembers. 'He just wanted to be in show business of some sort. That was an opening, because he couldn't get a job in a band.'

Graham Silcock, a guitarist in Sharplin's band, added, 'He used to watch Tom playing at King Creole's. He was DJing and I used to see him standing at the side, just looking. That look as if, "Some day, man."'

Sharplin was fully aware of Russell's ambition, and did his best to help by lending some of his band members to help him on his way. His first song would be called 'I Just Want to be Like Marlon Brando'. As song titles go, it was hardly subtle, but his short-lived solo music career was his first proper acting gig as well – because what was his bizarre alter ego Russell le Roq if not a performance?

His new moniker came from a nickname given to him during his time as a DJ. Russell le Roq was a heightened, if at times sometimes accurate, version of the Russell Crowe we know now. Wearing his self-belief proudly on his clothes – in this case literally with his leather jacket bearing the name Russ emblazoned on the back – he was a cocksure, confident and sometimes embarrassing persona.

Terence O'Neill-Joyce, boss of Ode Records who signed him, remembered, '[He had] more confidence than the rest of the people I was dealing with put together.

'He had an innocence about him... he was just a nice person.'

Despite his confidence, Russell's debut single didn't

scratch, never mind dent, the music charts. Only played twice on local radio, it went on to sell just 500 copies.

Adding new members to the band, including Graham Silcock, they were soon called Russ le Roq and the Romantics. The new extended name followed another single, 'Pier 13' – which only sold 100 copies.

Their next single, 'Never Let Ya Slide', saw Russell's alter ego turn from brooding Brando wannabe to a more jokey persona. On the back of the sleeve, the handwritten note read, 'This is Roq & Roll music. It is not a rock 'n' roll revival disc. Anyone caught saying it is will be murdered by death, or shot by hanging or... forced to play session on my next record!!!'

This single too failed to make any impact, so Russell decided to seek out a member of The Car Crash Set, Trevor Reekie, to produce his fourth song, 'Shattered Glass'. Russell felt the band's sound wasn't dynamic enough to capture a bigger audience – hence the need for Reekie, who overhauled the band's sound with a funkier beat.

'We tried to jazz this piece of shit up and it didn't work at all,' Reekie remembers. 'It didn't work at all, but he was a laugh. He was so uncool that he was actually cooler than most of the so-called cool people. He was kind of a freak, but he used to get away with it. It was a bullshit time and Russ was for real. He used to walk around with this jacket that had Russ on the back. He had so much bottle.'

Russell's parents gave as much as they could to help him, offering their savings to help his quest. But it was clear that even with his self-confidence, the band were surely consigned to nothing more than a footnote in New Zealand music history.

'He used to say he was doing really well,' Silcock said, 'and the other guys and I looked at each other – "If you say so, great." If we were doing that well, we never made much out of it. We used to see the records in these old bins for 50 cents. My friends used to remind me of that.'

Russell now decided to invest in a different enterprise – an under-age night club in Auckland called The Venue. Despite trouble from youths who were moved into the area from nearby Aotea Square by police, he was convinced the club would be a success – a place that the coolest bands would attend.

Reekie remembers, 'We used to rehearse there with the Car Crash Set sometimes. It was an under-age nightclub and it was in the wrong part of town, so cool people didn't go there. It must have been hard work. I doubt if he made any money out of it.'

Youth magazine *Rip It Up* reported in 1984 that the venue was closing down, writing, 'Financial problems have caused The Venue to go under, nine months after it opened ... le Roq said lower than expected numbers caused initial problems in covering overheads and when The Venue had to close down for two weeks in August, because of violence from outsiders, it dealt finances a death blow – not a pleasant experience.'

Reluctantly giving up his dream of owning music

venues, Russell was briefly an entertainments officer at the Pakota Island resort in the Hauraki Gulf – a stint that didn't last long after he was fired for livening up the bingo call with the words, 'Number one: up your bum.'

Another attempt at conquering the pop charts, with a guitarist named Dean Cochrane on the song 'What's the Difference', would see him failing again to become a music star.

A break arrived when two stage producers turned up in Auckland looking for actors to add local flavour to their production of the *Rocky Horror Show*. The cult production was big news in the stage world, offering an open invitation to the audience to join in with the flamboyant, camp atmosphere by dressing up in suspenders and ghoulish make-up.

Wilton Morley and Peter Davis were delighted with its success after buying the stage rights in the 1980s and, while retaining the same actors for the main parts, they were always on the lookout for new blood in the supporting roles. 'We found Russell in a band in Auckland and hired him,' Davis remembered.

So Russell got the part and discovered, for the first time in his life, that acting could be a legitimate career move. 'I'm fundamentally quite shy,' he said, 'so that thing of taking on another character is quite a liberating thing to do, because within that character framework you can now go to all these other places. And I never found another job that I was actually that good at.'

Talking about the show, he added, 'It's high camp, absolutely. But if it's played without reality it's completely meaningless – it's just people grinding away in stockings.'

Russell still hadn't given up his dreams of being a pop star just yet – forming Roman Antix with guitarist Cochrane and his *Rocky Horror Show* co-star Mark Rimington. He struck up a relationship with Rimington after they both jumped queues at the *Rocky Horror* audition.

The Russell Crowe that Rimington met was blessed with a raw but obvious acting talent – he 'couldn't sing to save himself. But he had great presence. He was unbearably arrogant and rubbed people the wrong way. He was so determined to become somebody.'

The band would tour their local areas playing new songs and old. 'I had to shadow-sing him when we were doing the tour, to keep him in tune,' said Rimington. 'He never said he was a great singer, but he was a great front man. He knew how to do a show.'

Despite their close time together, Rimington's memory of the actor paints him as 'driven' and 'arrogant'. He added, 'Whatever he was focused on, it was at the expense of anything else. The women fell by the wayside pretty quickly. If people had a use, he would certainly find it. I wouldn't describe him as the most caring person in the world.'

Morley came to see Russell following an impressive start on *Rocky Horror*. It was there that Morley convinced him that he should give up his music dream and focus on honing his acting talents. '[He] suggested that I was wasting my time in New Zealand,' Russell said. 'He told me, one, stop playing in a band and concentrate on acting and two, come to Australia where he would have employment for me.'

And so Russell headed back to Australia with dreams of making it as an actor.

CHAPTER THREE

CROWE FLYING SOLO

'From the beginning he was determined to be a star.'
– Former manager Martin Bedford

Alas, Australia at that moment wasn't to be. In fact, Russell was to move back to New Zealand, going on to act in over 450 performances of the *Rocky Horror Show*, starting off with the dual character of Eddie and Dr Scott. The 19-year-old actor was revelling in his surroundings. He was getting a great apprenticeship with seasoned professional actors, and because he was treading the boards, he was learning to think on his feet and understand what was needed to get an audience involved. He was soon promoted to the plum role of Frank N Furter – the role made famous by Tim Curry in the film version.

'I did 458 performances,' Russell recalled in *Interview* magazine in 1997. 'I was Eddie and Dr Scott for about 400 performances and about 58 as Frank N Furter. I was the understudy [for Frank] when the understudy's nightmare came true. I actually had to go on without any rehearsal; I didn't even bother to try out my shoes. I figured the other guy would do his gig. I only agreed to it because it was an extra $50 a week. So, suddenly, bang! I'm on as Frank.'

Davis and Morley were delighted with their find, with Davis saying, 'We found Russell in a band in Auckland and hired him. You could say a star was born.'

Russell added, 'Right through my childhood, and then into sort of my early twenties and everything, I really had no idea with the acting stuff. I never really focused on it, because music was my priority. Then basically somebody gave me an important job and asked me to treat it seriously. And when I treated it seriously I realised that I could really disappear inside this, you know?'

Next up was *Blood Brothers*, one of the longest running shows in the London West End. It saw a number of events that would be repeated ad nauseam in Russell's career – the critical raves and the sudden burst of anger at a moment's notice.

With critics calling his performance 'strong' and 'convincing' he was revelling in the role, but there was never a chance that Russell would rest on his laurels – and his stage intensity once again ruffled feathers.

His co-star Peter Cousens was furious night after night of the production. It was all due to one scene, which saw Russell fire a shot at him. 'When the gun goes off, it should fly across the stage, but Russell never controlled it and it always hit me,' recalled Cousens.

'We were at loggerheads from the start. He was terrific, but erratic. He lacked discipline and wasn't familiar with theatre etiquette. One night when the gun landed on me yet again I blew my top, marched into his dressing room and called him an arrogant amateur.

'He tried to punch me, but the guys in the dressing room held him back. He was hurling abuse and finally broke free and head-butted me in the face. Blood poured out – the bastard had broken my nose.'

Despite playing brothers in the production, they couldn't have been further removed in real life: Russell, the actor who works from the gut and unrestrained instinct; Cousens, an experienced stage actor and drama school graduate.

Being faced with warring co-stars after only a month was a headache producer and director Danny Hillier didn't need. But they weren't the first actors to trade blows, nor would they be the last. He was convinced some breathing room was needed for the two, and ordered them to each write an apology note to the other.

An apology from Cousens, who had to attend his own daughter's christening with black eyes, was swiftly penned, but nothing was forthcoming from Russell. A production source told the *Sunday Times* magazine, 'The producer was furious with Crowe. The producer was the type of person you don't fuck with, but Russell fucked with everyone.'

That weekend, Hillier had no choice but to fire the young actor.

The set-back hurt Russell deeply – and shaking the brazen actor back into life would take some time. It's unclear whether it was his actions leading to the incident or the fact that he wasted an opportunity that was such a burning disappointment – perhaps both.

However, he would always think back to a note penned on a school friend's wall. It simply read, 'How badly do you want it?' The friend was Simon Prast, who would go on to be a director of the Auckland Theatre Company. He explained: 'This was, of course, a reference to becoming an actor. Clearly, he wanted it reasonably badly!'

That was in no doubt, with Rimington adding, 'I'm absolutely certain he always wanted to be a star. I don't know why. I don't think it was money. He could have always done a job at any time that could have made him more money. So, as to what actually drives a person to do that… I have no idea.'

At this point, Russell was living in a two-bedroomed flat full of cockroaches and empty crates that had been crammed with alcohol. Speaking in 1989, Russell said, 'Well, when I first arrived in Sydney, I spent 22 weeks in this grotty $50-a-week place with just a bed and a cupboard and the toilet halfway down the corridor. For the first time my parents were some distance away. I did a lot of thinking and realised I really appreciated what my father had instilled in me.

'A lot of people think that because there is a dole there they should use it and that there are a lot of ways to misuse the system. I believe in singing for my supper. I'll never accept a grant because what I do should be able to be founded purely on free enterprise.'

Stints busking and street performing barely helped him make ends meet, but Russell the waiter didn't last very long. 'This American woman asked me for a decaffeinated coffee. In New Zealand in 1986 if you asked for a coffee it was a teaspoon of Nescafé. I come over here and suddenly I'm faced with long black, short black, cappuccino, coffee latte and decaffeinated. So I take her a cup of hot water. And she says, "Russell, this is just boiling water," and I say, "Lady, when we decaffeinate something in Australia we don't fuck around." She complained to the management.' He was fired straight away.

To make ends meet Russell would live off tacos, drink with the alcoholics nearby and busk constantly with his old friend Dean Cochrane.

When his family came to visit him they were shocked by what they saw. 'We used to go to Sydney, take him out and give him a good feed,' his gran recalled. 'My goodness, he'd be on the bare bones of his bum, you had to help him. But he wouldn't give up.'

Russell would busk all over the city, playing rock 'n' roll songs and bantering with passers-by – all with one eye open for the police so they could make a hasty exit if spotted. Wearing his usual busking combo of jeans and white T-shirt with a cigarette placed self-consciously behind his ear, he would entertain crowds, chat up girls and occasionally get into a fight.

A Norwegian backpacker called Trude remembers Russell coming to her rescue following a brief introduction in a bar. 'We were just about to leave when these three really creepy guys sort of surrounded me and my friend. They were really horrible and threatening and started to say what they would like to do with us. We didn't know what to do and one of them sort of grabbed me and tried to kiss me. I reached to try to push him off but just then there was a flash of movement from behind and the guy slid to the floor.

'I got a glimpse of Russell with his arm out and I realised he had hit the guy. His two friends just disappeared. Russell seemed to be on his own but they weren't about to tangle with him. He said, "Sorry about that. Are you all right?"'

They ended up dating for several weeks but parted because she went back to her travels. 'I'm not at all surprised he has made it so big in movies. He's a fabulous guy.'

At the time, Russell was frustrated at the Australian film industry, saying in 1989, 'Do you know what killed this business in the first place? A lot of people who didn't understand what passion was, who didn't give a zip about art but thought, "Gee whizz, I can get a great tax break here. I'll make a movie." We ended up with a whole lot of shit and we're still recovering from that.'

With Australia not making the kind of films that he wanted to do – at that time anyhow – it was clearly Hollywood he had his sights set on. A conversation with his agent, Shirley Pearce, early in his career, went like this: 'Shirley said, "What is it you want to achieve?" And I said, "Well, have you seen *Rain Man*?" which had just come out. And she said, "Yes..." and I said, "Well, that sort of work..." and Shirley said, "What, like Tom Cruise?" and I said, "No, the other fella."'

Russell was at a crossroads. He had tasted the highs of performing on stage but, living off a meagre $3.50 a day, these were the low times.

CHAPTER FOUR

EVERYBODY NEEDS GOOD NEIGHBOURS

'I never realised the actor he'd become.'
– Ian Smith (Harold Bishop)

It was just another morning for Russell in his small Sydney flat when he stopped in his kitchen and sat down on a chair. A bird hovered outside before setting down on his windowsill. The bird, a rare kookaburra, looked him in the eye and it was then that Russell get a strange sensation – a feeling that something had happened to his beloved grandfather.

He rushed to the phone to call his parents, and was told that Stan had died. 'I insisted the bird was my grandfather's spirit, but my mom would have nothing of it.' Later, she would break down in tears when a family friend also revealed that a bird visited her that same day.

The death was a crushing blow to Russell. He had adored his grandfather and had even saved what little money he had to take Stan out for a meal when he'd visited Sydney six months earlier. 'My grandfather came to Australia to try to explain to me that he was dying. I was a young kid, very much into myself at the time. I was busking on the streets, just to make enough money to pay my rent. There was this Japanese restaurant I'd always wanted to eat at, but couldn't afford, so I suggested we go there.'

It ended up being a costly misfire as the smells in the Japanese restaurant brought back painful memories for Stan of his time in the war. 'We couldn't have the talk he wanted to,' he said sadly.

His grandfather had been something of a mentor to Russell, with Joy noting that her late husband and grandson were so alike. When she'd first met Stan all those years ago, she had wrongly perceived his ambition and fierce ambition as arrogance – something that has tarred Russell for many years. Joy gave Russell her late husband's World War II medals and his prized camera, as well as a selection of his famed war stills.

The devastated Russell was a mess. He had lost his grandfather and he had been axed from *Blood Brothers*. A brief flirtation with the idea of enrolling at Sydney's National Institute For Dramatic Arts – a highly regarded drama school which counted Mel Gibson among its former students – came to nothing after he realised he was learning so much through on-the-job experience and he didn't want to lose that momentum. But the more he performed on stage in Melbourne and

Sydney the more he felt that it was on screen that his future lay.

In a 1997 interview, he said, 'Theatre was my driving ambition in life as a young man. I couldn't think of anything more magical than working in an Arthur Miller play at the Sydney Opera House. But the film director, George Ogilvie, offered me a chance to work in a film. It takes a real specialist, a theatrical performer like Geoffrey Rush, to make sure the guy in the 40th row of a live theatre house gets it. I never felt in my heart of hearts I could achieve that. I had never imagined making movies then because I didn't think anyone would want me to be in their movie. Once I got onto a movie set, I realised this was my medium.

'Because what I discovered in the process was I had no limitations as an actor in the cinema. After George saw me in a number of theatre roles he said, "You're going to make a great cinema actor."'

At this point Russell had already managed to land a role in two popular Australian TV shows. The first was an appearance in the courtroom drama *Rafferty's Rules*, and this was followed by a four-episode stint in the long-running soap opera *Neighbours*.

Because of his stage work, Russell had signed on with the agency Bedford and Pearce, but he was still reluctant about starring in the soap as petty thief Kenny. 'I was reading the script and I'm thinking, "This is awful." Then I get to the last scene and I've got to punch Craig

McLachlan, and Jason Donovan's trying to break up the fight while Kylie Minogue is riding on my back trying to strangle me. And I went, "Yes, I'll do it."'

'I did four episodes of *Neighbours* in 1987, and four episodes of *Neighbours* takes about 25 minutes to shoot because they work a pretty tight schedule. I got more money for that four days' work than I got for the whole season at Melbourne Theatre.'

Ian Smith, who played Harold Bishop, said he'd been surprised at Russell's subsequent success. 'I never realised the actor he'd become. I really didn't get to know Russell that much. He wasn't with us that long.'

But Russell was desperate to be in films, and he was to get his wish in *Blood Oath*. The World War II courtroom drama, which told the true story of an Australian military lawyer's job to prosecute Japanese war criminals, featured a small part for Russell – but it was a foot in the door nonetheless. He would be teaming up with his *Neighbours* sparring partner Jason Donovan – who was hoping that this film would show he was more than just a soap actor and pop star.

The film starred Bryan Brown, a popular leading man in Australia at that time. Russell's role was very much in the background with Brown in the foreground. Not that Russell cared very much. His audition had impressed the film's casting director, who hadn't expected such an intense and energetic audition for that part.

Russell recalled of his screen time, 'I just walked

around the back carrying Bryan's pencils. "Pencil, Mr Brown?" It's hard to look like you're not trying to get your head in the shot.'

When an interviewer asked him if he was ever tempted to do just that, he snapped, 'No, of course not. Don't be stupid. I tell you though, I learnt a hell of a lot on that set. It was my first feature and Bryan was great.'

In the TV special *Russell Crowe: Behind The Gladiator*, he recalled, 'I got to work with him [Brown] for about 10 weeks and watch him, observe him and ask him lots of questions. It was kind of cool, because the major work I had done before that in terms of acting was about professional work on the stage – you know, stage musicals – so it was a really different environment.'

It was clear he loved working with Brown, and he showed a willingness to learn despite his reputation.

'To get fit for the part Russell would run miles and miles in ridiculous heat,' said John Clarke, the film's script editor and an actor in the film. 'We would be travelling to and from the set in vehicles and we would pass Russell, looking magnificent and bathed in sweat, pounding the roads.'

One anecdote burned in Russell's mouth as much as it did his mind. It happened during first day of filming. 'As I came walking out of the jungle,' he said, 'I decided I'd smoke a cigarette, which is fine. The only problem is that they didn't shoot the scene only once, they shot it 27 times from all number of angles. At the end my throat was killing me. Bryan Brown asked me what I'd learned that day and I said, "Never smoke a cigarette in a scene."'

Blood Oath – or *Prisoners of the Sun* as it would also be known – performed only averagely at the box office. It would signal the end of Donovan's attempt to become a movie star but for Russell it was just the beginning.

CHAPTER FIVE

LEADING FROM THE FRONT

'I always wanted to play that laid-back Aussie male who has an emotional outpouring.'

– Russell Crowe

It had only been a small part in *Blood Oath*, but all actors have to start somewhere. But Russell's real movie debut should have been *The Crossing*.

The 1950s coming-of-age movie would in fact be Russell's second picture. It was originally due to be made before he secured the role in *Blood Oath*, but the shooting dates were pushed back.

Russell remembers of the audition. 'George Ogilvie sat 16 young people in a room, eight girls and eight guys, and said, "It's nine o'clock in the morning. At the end of the day, around five o'clock, I'm going to know who's going to play the lead role in my film."

'I got home and I get a phone call and it's George and he says to me, "I think you have a great career in the cinema ahead of you. Which role would you like to play?" I chose Johnny because I felt his journey had far more emotional turns.'

Explaining the day-long workshop auditions, the director said, 'If you spend 15 minutes with an actor you can get only a superficial idea of what they can do. So a whole day workshopping relaxes them, and finally you can see what they can do.'

Russell was understandably delighted. As he put it, 'I started in the business at six and I didn't get that role in *The Crossing* until I was 26. So in between, even though I was working continuously in the theatre, that represents thousands of failed auditions for movies. It was just a huge thing.'

Faith Martin, who was casting director on the film, recalled to the *Sydney Morning Herald* in 2001, 'Russell was very intense, highly intelligent and he drew you to him.'

Ogilvy added, 'This is not specifically in looks but Russell reminds me of James Dean in the way that he has the charisma Dean had. He's the sort of actor you watch work and you have no idea what he'll do next. That's rare, that mystery about him.

'There was a sort of hunger in Russell's eyes. Most young actors want to please. It can be a barrier. Russell didn't want to please. He wanted to be that role.'

The film tells the tale of a love triangle set in the Australian outback in the 1950s. Robert Mammone plays Sam – a young man who leaves his home town to make a life in the city. He returns a year and a half later to persuade Meg, the girl that he left behind, to come with him to the city. Complications arise from the fact that she has since embarked on a love affair with Sam's best friend, Johnny (Russell Crowe).

Talking about his character, Russell said, 'Johnny's simplicity is part of his complexity and he has an ability to communicate his feelings to her, which is so Australian. He's a product of his environment and he wants to progress within it, to marry Meg and have a family, with all the stability that represents. He's tied to the town through his mother and his dead father.'

Mammone said, 'I didn't think I'd have a chance of getting it. I didn't see myself in that role. I was just going for a supporting role. I was in the workshops and I was the oldest person there. They were trying to work out whether they wanted young actors or to get older actors to play younger roles. They decided on actors who were a bit older because they felt the young actors didn't have the life experience.'

Russell's leading lady would be Danielle Spencer, an actress with whom he would have an early relationship, rekindle their passion many years later and go on to marry.

'I knew it was a great role and I was determined to get it,' she said at the time. 'I liked the story, the fact that it was a love triangle, and my character has a lot of strength. On the one hand she was a real farm girl, an innocent leading a simple life, but emotionally she's more complicated – decisions, especially when it comes to Johnny and Sam, are not cut and dried for her.

'Johnny's lovable and Sam's exciting, so it's a difficult choice for Meg. For Johnny, things are simple. He wants to marry Meg and that's it. He knows what he is about, but Sam is attractive because he is a dreamer.'

Ogilvie made sure his three main cast members spent time together. 'We had three weeks rehearsal,' Russell explained. 'Instead of blocking out the scenes, we just discussed things and played games, but in that time we had every single part of our character indelibly printed in our minds. We became the characters without having to speak the dialogue.'

Mammone added, 'We talked to each other throughout the shoot, questioning certain aspects of our character and how they affect one another.'

'The director of *The Crossing* introduced us and then the film was postponed for about three months but we kept in touch during that time,' Spencer remembered. 'The three of us would do things like go to the gym together, so we formed a bond before we even went on the set. I thought Russell was great fun and we really have him to thank for us all becoming so close because he was the one who initiated most of the outings. It's always important to him to try and establish a good, solid relationship with people he is working with.'

Russell also did some research for the part, heading over to a farm in New South Wales, where he learnt how to shear sheep. He also made sure he had a say in what the character would wear. 'When I did *The Crossing* the costume people wanted me to wear a leather jacket and pretend I was James Dean. I said, "It's in the bush, right? I'm a shearer, I've never been out of this town. How the fuck did I get a leather jacket?"'

One of the early scenes, of the pair making love in the hay in a barn featured a passionate clinch that would be repeated off camera. Afterwards, Danielle was said to have told a member of a crew, 'I didn't know a man could kiss a girl quite like that.'

It was to be the start of something special between the pair, although she glossed over it at first. 'I had a boyfriend back in Sydney and when you have a crew around it's very difficult to get involved in the sexual aspect of the scene because it's sort of embarrassing. It was a closed set, but it was still very nerve-racking – we were both very nervous and self-conscious. Russell is obviously an attractive guy but I wasn't thinking along those lines at that point because it was a big movie for both of us and we were very focused on that.'

During the making of *The Crossing*, Ogilvie told Russell that he had to replace his missing tooth – the result of a rugby match at school when he was 10 years old. 'He was very nice about it,' Russell recalled. 'He listened to it all, and said, "All right, let me put it this way, Russell. You're playing the lead character in my film, right? The character of Johnny has two front teeth."

'I told him that I just didn't want anything false going on here and I went through my whole teenage years, how I failed these auditions, never got a TV commercial, and how all the jobs I got were with this gap in my teeth. George just said, "Well, I think it's good to grow out of that behaviour. Let's have two front teeth when we play Johnny Ryan, shall we?" So I got a new tooth.'

He would add later, 'The truth is, I don't know very well why I was so stubborn about not fixing them. It was like losing a hand – you have to get used to life's losses and scars. Those broken teeth were part of who I was. But the funny thing was that I'd been acting in theatre for 12 years, because back then I didn't think about becoming a movie actor. My ambition was to make a good career in theatre, and I had been working, like I said, for many years with a broken mouth and I had even done some movies by the time I had the teeth fixed.

'And from then on, my movie career took off. Which doesn't say much for the movie industry, of course. But later I thought about it a lot and I think it was a real blessing for me being scarred until I was 27, because that allowed me time to grow, to learn to act.'

Ogilvie now admits, 'I wasn't immediately taken with him. He had a very "I'm Russell Crowe, who are you?" attitude. He was very polite, very gracious, but he made no efforts to please me at all.'

However, in Ogilvie, Russell had found a director who gave him the sort of freedom that he needed. 'In *The*

Crossing, George let me take risks. He let me be wild and go for it because he trusted me. Other directors frame a shot and say, "Don't bloody move!" If you move outside the script they say, "Cut!" I think once you're inside the character, let it come out. People try to stop you and that's hard. George said right from the moment we met he trusted my instincts.'

Russell has been at great pains in the past to clear up misconceptions about him – about his reputation for being difficult on set. He rationalises that he's difficult in terms of making sure the film is good as can be – something that is backed up by actors and directors he has worked with. One actress confided to this author privately that during filming of one of his biggest movies, 'He would ask to re-do scenes over and over again, sometimes doing more than 40 takes unnecessarily and there was a feeling that [the director] was letting him direct the film.'

However, Russell has always insisted that it's the 'director's medium'. Talking to *Inside The Actors Studio*, he said, 'I make movies and I'm working for that particular person. So if I can't find common ground with that person on a particular subject, or aspect of the character, then I let it go. Because I'm making his movie. Yes, I'm playing the character and all that sort of stuff, but you've gotta allow for the fact that it isn't your gig. You know, you're just lucky enough to be on the bus. It's his gig. His or her gig.

'Many times you have a situation where something that you said wasn't listened to or whatever, and then you get a call from the editing room going, "Fuck, I wish I'd listened to what you said, 'cause that's exactly what's missing," you know? So you have those kinda conversations but they're – they're pleasant.

'It's not, not, not a fight. I'm not there to have arguments of that nature with a film director. So, your choice of who you're gonna work with is very important on that level. I like to work with directors who are really confident about their point of view.

'If they're confident on who they are as a director and what and how they approach the medium then they're not threatened when you come up with an idea as an actor. You gotta be fluid enough to correct yourself. If something you assumed about a character early on is wrong and you find yourself out, just let the fucking thing go! Let it go! Drop it, you know?

'Wasting time on a film set is not your privilege. Being on the film set is your privilege.'

In *The Crossing*, Russell was allowed to trust his instinct, and the instinct in Russell is feral and visceral. He digs deep and is not frightened by what he discovers there. 'I get really passionate about what I do,' admits Russell. 'Some people get threatened by that, threatened by the passion. George doesn't. So you pump it out for George and all he says is, "Give me some more." So you do. You reach in and pull it out.'

The advantage of having three relative unknowns as your leading characters is that it gives the film an edge – a blank slate for the audience about who they are watching. There are no pre-conceived notions about who these actors are, so it's easier to get into their characters and the world they live in.

The disadvantage, of course, is their lack of experience being on a movie set. It's a sink or swim environment. And that's why Ogilvie, who was an actor himself, was a calming and authoritative presence on set – always at hand to offer advice and the experience but knowing when to leave them alone to work it out for themselves.

During one difficult scene, Russell recounted, Ogilvie took him aside. 'And at this point I really didn't know his history and then I find out later that he was this fabulous actor and when he became a director he decided he was going to make a 100 per cent switch. So he goes, "I can't explain it so I am just going to do it." So we are just standing in this car park and he just, on a dime, bang! The most radiant, deep, emotional series of information coming at me and that was an incredible lesson.'

Reviews of the film were generally positive, with Russell receiving the majority of the praise. *Sydney Morning Herald* thought the film was 'too eager to impress' but reserved praise for Russell's performance.

'But the true revelation is Crowe, in his first major film role,' the review read. 'In most movies like this one, the boyfriend/fiancé/husband is usually either an overbearing jerk who causes the heroine much unhappiness, or an annoying sap whose constant declarations of love sound laughingly hollow. But when Johnny professes his love for Meg, it's clear that he means it. And when he is threatened with losing her, he reacts not with physical violence or menace, but instead seems to unravel at his own emotional seams. Crowe takes a character that could have been one-note and creates one who is masculine and practical, yet sensitive enough to know that his way of life is in danger and there's really nothing he can do about it.'

It was also a role for which Russell received a nomination for Best Actor at the AFI (Australian Film Institute) awards. It had taken him years to get there but Russell had starred in a film and he had passed with flying colours.

'When I first saw it, I thought it was a very beautiful film and I am very proud of director George Ogilvie and his achievements,' he said of his first leading role. 'I don't think it worked commercially because, despite its universal themes, a lot of people couldn't relate to its rural setting.'

However, it's one that meant a lot to him – and he has stayed friends with both Mammone and Ogilvie. In fact, Mammone was one of Russell's groomsmen at his wedding to Danielle, while Ogilvie was a guest.

CHAPTER SIX

RUSSELL GETS SPOTTED

'I really like him because he's ballsy, he's got guts and he's macho.'

– Sir Anthony Hopkins

Rave reviews and an award nomination were a good start for Russell as a leading man. It was a vindication he desperately needed. You can only go on swaggering self-confidence for so long before you need confirmation from elsewhere. He got that from *The Crossing*. The *Daily Mirror* singled out him as one to watch, adding, 'He's the actor I predict will become not just a screen heart-throb but a first class performer.'

Russell took home a poster of the film and stuck it on his wall. There was a touch of the 'Hey, look at me' factor about it, but it would be a motivational tool, proving that if you work hard enough, big things can happen. The next role for Russell was of extreme importance. He needed something of stature before he would accept it.

It wasn't necessarily leading roles that he was looking

for. As long as the script was good, he'd consider the part. 'The bottom line is I just love my job,' he said in 2009. 'I love to create a character, I love to go to work, I like to be on a film set. All the other stuff that goes with acting, that's all stuff that I've had to learn to deal with, but learning my dialogue, deciding what the character is going look like, walk like: I love doing that stuff. I can do that everyday of my life for the rest of my life and I am as happy as Larry.'

The script that intrigued him the most was for *Proof* – a touching drama about Martin, a blind man, who strikes up a relationship with a dishwasher named Andy. When Martin's housekeeper, Cecilia, has her romantic advances rejected, she sets upon romancing Andy in a bid to drive a wedge between the two men.

'It was a fantastic script,' Russell said. 'It was the best script I've ever read as far as its completeness is concerned, because it's quite a complicated concept. [Director] Jocelyn [Moorhouse] takes it through and explains everything to the audience just when they need to know exactly what the hell is going on. The simple fact is, as soon as I read it, I knew I wanted to do it.'

It was to be Moorhouse's directorial debut, so strangely enough it would be Russell taking a risk on her, rather than the other way round. He had a chance to make a name for himself and he didn't want to upset the momentum started by *The Crossing*, nor did he want to just turn up agreeing to every script that went his way.

It was something that set him apart from other budding actors. He had the movie star looks – albeit less 'pretty boy' and more imposing and masculine – but he was determined to have a body of work that reflected that of a character actor. And his resumé – his Russ le Roq singing career aside – has a better hit rate than others. He has managed to pick scripts that are interesting to him, but more admirably – or through good fortune – he generally managed to do that before he became successful. *Proof,* in which he shows warmth as the amiable Andy, is the perfect example.

'It's all about a search for truth and honesty,' Russell said of the movie. 'Love is also a theme, although it's a very strange sort of love. Jocelyn Moorhouse is not your average director. She's got a very intense imagination and an extremely oblique level of observation. She seems to be able to find something new in old themes. She sees another dimension.

'My character, Andy, has rebelled from his middle-class background. He's a bit rootless and directionless. But he has made himself that way. But Andy gets stuck in a lot of things, you know? I hate people like that. He gets caught and can't work his way out, the son of a bitch. I enjoyed playing Andy.

'When you read a lot of scripts, you know the difference between a good one and a bad one. When you're talking about the situation where the writer is actually going to direct you, one can be very confident that the subtleties contained in that script will come out, because they come out of her head. Jocelyn and I are pretty similar in some ways. She's really committed and passionate with a unique creativity. All of those things tend to add up to possibly fiery moments, but we had one of those relationships where every single small point we discussed we went through. Of course we were bound to disagree on a number of things, but all that happened is that, through those conversations we hit upon the best idea, not just one idea or an option and that's the way I like to work.'

Proof was originally intended to be a short film, but the director was told that the 50-minute story – which transpired from a conversation with a friend about a blind relative who took pictures and had someone describe what he took – was too long. She would struggle to get funding and should think about making it a feature-length film.

Talking on the DVD commentary, Hugo Weaving (who played Martin) told about his experiences working with Russell. 'I'd been warned about working with Russell because I'd talked to an actor that worked with him on stage and had a bit of a run-in with him. He said, "Oh, you have to watch out for him, mate." But we got on very well. He was immensely charming and it's an immensely charming performance too.

'He was very positive, energetic, he's intelligent, he's good fun. We had a good time working together and also off-set. And he was determined to read to me everyday because he thought that was something Andy would do for Martin. So Russell used to read me – I don't know why – from this book on the French Revolution. So I used to sit and listen to Russell telling me all about the French Revolution every day, during rehearsals and sometimes on set as well. Pretty bizarre, really.'

Russell was again nominated by the AFI in 1991 – this time receiving the Best Supporting Actor award. The film would go on to win six more honours at the awards, including best film, director, script and actor for Weaving. The film's success at the ceremony transferred to the box office, expanding from four screens in Australian cinemas to nearly 30.

Talking about his award win to *Juice Magazine* in 1993, Russell said, 'I really like that stuff. I loved watching the Academy Awards when I was a kid. And that three seconds when they read my name for *Proof*, I really enjoyed it. There's always this thing with being an actor. Are you actually an actor, or one of the multitude of pretenders? You gotta ask yourself.'

Russell was given another boost when he heard that the film was to be shown at that year's Cannes Film Festival. It han't originally impressed the festival advisors but after seeing the final cut they decided to show it – and it was well received by the press. *Film Link* wrote, 'Razor sharp, blackly comic and keenly intelligent, *Proof* is one of the best Australian film of the 1990s.' They would also praise Russell's performance as 'excellent', while the *New York Times* said he was 'eager and lithe'.

So off he went to France to mingle with the very biggest names of the Hollywood industry. Cannes is a byword for everything that is glamorous and luxurious about the film industry. For nearly two weeks, the city is awash with large yachts, the glitziest parties, the biggest names and light bulbs flashing everywhere from the world's media.

For Russell, it was something of a culture shock, but while he soaked up the going-ons it only made him even more sure that he wanted to amass an impressive body of work rather than jump at the first chance of Hollywood. Ironically it also fuelled his belief that Hollywood was where he would end up. And it was a genuine Hollywood star that he would work with next in *Spotswood*.

He would star alongside Sir Anthony Hopkins, something that was a joyous experience for Russell. 'I already knew that he was a great actor, so that wasn't a surprise. The fact that he's a great person was an added bonus. He's an extremely nice guy and exceedingly professional, and I think what I learnt from him the most was that great actors remain generous.

'He showed me the power of detail. Hopkins could map out a 20-point journey with a coffee cup. I've seen him pick up a coffee cup, and every time he picks it up, he is doing something different. But nothing that he is doing with the coffee cup is distracting from his eyes, from the internal process.'

Hopkins was quick to return the compliment. 'One of the people I got to know years ago, which was a great privilege, was Laurence Olivier. He seemed to be like a racing driver as an actor. He was like a laser – that was his power. And the only actor I've met since who had that quality of laser-like determination is Russell Crowe.

'The first day I started working with him. I thought, "That guy's got it!" The best way to describe Russell is like a shark: he's a shark circling round. You could see it in the way he was figuring things out. Just before he became the big hit in *L.A. Confidential*, I was asked if I would do a film interview about him.

'They asked me about him, and I said, "Oh yeah, I could see it in him." He was different from the other guys. He was argumentative. He argued with the director all the time. And I said to the director, "Listen to him, he's got a point."'

It's no surprise the pair got on so well. Like Russell, Hopkins has always been something of a cinematic drifter and one who had trouble early on in his career with where to channel his obvious talents.

In 2006 *Total Film* asked Hopkins if he saw a lot of his younger self in Russell and he said, 'Yeah I did. There's a photograph of me here from 1970. This young lady gave it to me and I looked at it and I thought, "I was a bad boy then." I thought, "God, this is an unhappy camper" but boy! I'd take on anyone back then!'

He added, 'I don't know Russell that well, but I admire

and I really like him, because he's ballsy, he's got guts, he's macho and all the rest of it.'

Asked about Hopkins' perceived dismissing of the profession at the time, Russell said, 'You can take that as cynicism if you want, but I think it's more a protectionist thing. It happens to me a lot when people ask me about my preparation, which ultimately has nothing to do with anything, apart from what I give the performance. It's the performance that counts, which is what you judge. So whether I do five minutes preparation or five years, it doesn't mean anything, because what comes out of the screen later is what finally counts.

'Therefore I think Hopkins is possibly a little sick of going over and over that sort of thing, so he says: "This is my job." And it is a job, and it's damn hard work, because if you don't concentrate or put some effort in, nothing comes out. There isn't a secret of being a great actor that somebody can read in a magazine. You're born with it from the first time you open your mouth. You can get better or worse, but you either can or can't do it.'

Talking about *Spotswood* during shooting, Russell recalled, 'I play a small part as a slimy businessman. He's a bit of a bastard, a parody of ambition. I don't know if I've gone too far. I always think I go over the top with whatever I do. Mark Joffe doesn't give a lot of direction. He let me go. He said, "The camera is gonna be here and you are gonna be there. Now do something."

'The film as a whole is lovely and it made me smile. It's a very entertaining film.'

Russell was getting more and more offers, but again he decided he'd go for a supporting part in *Love in Limbo*, or *Great Pretender* as it was first known. 'I'm very choosy in what I do. I knocked back the lead role in one film which paid a lot more money in order to play a good support role in *Great Pretender*, because I didn't want the responsibility of a lead in that other film.'

The sweet coming-of-age film set in the 1950s tells the story of a young man named Ken trying to lose his virginity. Talking about his character, Russell said, 'I play Arthur, a Baptist Welshman, who's the warehouse supervisor where Ken works. His small amount of authority has really gone to his head, but through the course of the film, he spreads his wings a little bit, possibly to become a little bit more Australian, after having spent so many years in a closed Welsh environment.'

Russell had Hopkins to thank for the accent. On learning of the role, Russell asked the veteran actor for advice on how to master the accent, to which he simply replied, 'Do an Indian accent badly and you'll be close.' Russell would also take a trip to the country, dictaphone in hand, but later admitted, 'I really travelled to Wales to have a beer outside Cardiff Arms Park. That was my priority.'

Looking back at the character now, it is clear that it was one of his more interesting roles. 'It was the first time

I got to go haywire on screen. People are constantly telling me I should not be playing these little characters and say I'm wasting my face. But I laugh and say, "Hey, I'm an actor – this is what I physically look like."'

The character was far removed from the more intense ones that Russell would become known for – and he was remembered for being a fun presence on set.

Angela Roberts played Russell's mother in the film, and she remembers him as being cheeky and mischievous. 'He was a great guy and made us laugh by acting silly and ad-libbing. In the middle of a scene he would spot someone and say "Oh! You're in it too!"

'During a party scene when I was playing his mother, I had to look very stern and keep my eye on him, but he kept running over between dances and kissing me. He wasn't supposed to. His antics were totally out of the blue.

'He was like that with everyone. It was all good fun, and he made the cast feel at ease. He was just a normal person,' she added. 'You wouldn't have thought he was a star in the making.'

That may have been the case then, but his next film would remove any doubts.

CHAPTER SEVEN

RUSSELL CREATES A BUZZ

'I like villains because there's something so attractive about a committed person.'

– Russell Crowe

While *Love in Limbo* saw Russell showcasing a lighter side – and cast members enjoying a lighter side of Russell on set – there were still moments of unease. In this particular case, the cause was Russell relaxing between takes with a copy of Nazi reading material.

'It was funny actually, because halfway through that film I started preparing for *Romper Stomper*, so Aden Young [who played Barry] has all these photos of me in Arthur's silly old suits and ties reading *Mein Kampf*.'

He said, 'There's a sort of a filing system that you fill up and you empty. But stuff like reading *Mein Kampf*, it's nothing. I'm not reading it to take it in and believe in it, you know? I'm just reading it out of interest, and it focuses me, and through the act of reading I'm considering other aspects of the character as well.

'It kept me in an odd place. It kept me slightly unbalanced, and that's where I wanted to be while I was doing that role. A guy like [*Romper Stomper* skinhead] Hando is abhorrent to me. The philosophy that governs his life is something that disgusts me completely, so that was an interesting learning experience.'

Hando was a role that would burn into the consciousness of Australian film critics, cause an almighty fuss in the news media and create a buzz about Russell being one to watch in Hollywood. 'I didn't think they were going to make another movie like that in Australia for a long time,' he said.

Russell knew about the part for nearly 18 months before he landed it. The film's director Geoffrey Wright had been impressed after seeing his performance in *Proof*. 'I didn't know anything about Russell at the time. But I thought he was the most menacing gentle dishwasher I've ever seen. There's always something threatening about him on screen. Right after I'd seen *Proof* I called my producers and said, "We may have our boy."'

Up to that point, however, it looked as though Russell would miss his chance. Another actor had been cast – prompting Russell to phone the director repeatedly, insisting he had the wrong man. In the event, his casting was actually due to the original actor not looking fierce enough when they shaved his head. That wasn't the case with Russell. His already imposing frame, coupled with his hair shaved to the bone, was exactly the intense look that Wright was after for Hando, the leader of a group of Australian Nazi skinheads.

Typically, it was a part that he would immerse himself in. 'Every role has different things that speak to you. With *Romper Stomper*, I was afraid of delving into the darkness of the neo-Nazi ideology on one hand, but on the other hand, I could tell that it was going to be a very important social document. That was the imperative behind my doing it.'

To *HQ*, he added, 'The scary thing about my character, Hando, is the marriage of ultra-violence with ideology. Plus the unpredictability of it being just plain fucking mad. Racism is one of the most evil and heinous thought patterns that a human can get into. For that alone, it is important for me to do that character to demonstrate how wrong it is.'

Initially, while Russell liked the visceral energy from the script, he needed to make sure the film would capture the screenplay's tone. He even phoned the film's director, Geoffrey Wright, to ensure this wouldn't be a Nazi propaganda piece. 'He satisfied me. He's a very intelligent man. I could see the positive aspect of exposing this stuff to the public eye. National Socialism gets strength from being underground.'

In a revealing interview about his character, he said, 'What Hando is doing is standing up and saying, "I am strong enough to look after you. If you give me your loyalty I will solve all your little problems. Hang out with me, you'll never want for food, for money. I will organise the lot." He's the archetypal patriarch. And he loves these guys. People say a guy like that can't love – what a load of shit. He is creating a family, but the bottom line is the people who aren't in the family have to be wiped out.

'The perfect world for Hando is a situation where everyone is of the same mind. It's the idea that society would be more balanced and more easily controlled if everyone is the same. That's National Socialism. That's Hitler. That's racism.'

It was time spent in the UK that would prove to be a main source of inspiration for the character. Heading to Wrexham in Wales, where some of his relatives came from, with an English pal, he stopped off in Cardiff to try and perfect the accent for his *Love in Limbo* character. However, it turned out that his *Romper Stomper* character would benefit the most.

They stopped off at a pub, which was said to be filled with unsavoury characters. Russell strode in and saw that this was perfect place to do some research. Sitting down near a 'couple of Neanderthals' – according to his journalist friend Martyn Palmer – he quickly got into a conversation, ever so gently moving from small talk into more muddy waters. He was desperate for them to open up – and that they did, with 'spectacularly nasty racist garbage' coming from their mouths.

It was only later that Palmer realised just how much of a risk Russell had been taking – he'd been secretly taping them on his dictaphone. His recorder was also used when he went to watch Brighton & Hove Albion play Millwall in a football match. A pitch invasion at the end of the game had a clearly jubilant Russell grinning from ear to ear as he brandished his recorder and put it over his head, ensuring that every chant could be picked up – perfect for when he could play it over and over again, sometimes even drifting off to sleep with the lager-soaked hatred churning through his brain. And when he wasn't listening to football chants or Wagner, he would immerse himself in relevant reading material and surround himself with World War II memorabilia.

'With *Romper Stomper* and preparing for that character I made a decision that it couldn't be music, so for the first time I didn't have a guitar with me in the hotel room that I was staying in while we were shooting the movie. I had two cassette decks, or a cassette deck and a CD player, and I had a tape of white noise, and a CD of Wagner. I had one other cassette, which was a tape I had made in England of soccer crowds and that's all I listened to as Hando, and I could only listen to them together. I mean, like I couldn't have Wagner on by itself. It was either Wagner and the soccer crowd or Wagner and the white noise.

'And people would come and visit me when I was making that movie, and they were like, "Fucking weirdo. This dude's lost it, man. He's crazy." But it didn't seem to fit that while playing Hando I should be in my hotel room playing country and western songs. The whole thing about Hando – he wasn't a punk rocker, mate, he was a skinhead: he's a political animal. It's got nothing to do with music. And some people get the whole thing confused. For him he knew that music, he would know that music was played at their social events or whatever. He was a self-styled Führer, a leader of men – he wasn't going to be attracted by grubby little musicians. If he was going to listen to music he was going to listen to the pure Teutonic Wagner, not some fucking skanky punk band.

'We went from the politics of my role to the psychology of it. I even had to paint my own set of infantry soldiers,' he recalled.

Russell would work out regularly, desperate to bulk out for the role. His trainer, Greg Heasley, would use unorthodox methods during his training regime – which included him yelling, 'This one's for the Führer!' during punch-bag sessions.

'This guy was a massive help to me. He helped me understand the ideology behind the character I was playing,' he told *TV Weekly* in 1992. 'As I was doing bench presses in the gym, he'd be close to my ear saying, "You hate, you hate, you hate."'

He added, 'This was very hard for me to endure because I had to take on board all these elements, like fascism, that I abhor. I found that I was unable to sleep a lot of the time.'

The effort and preparation Russell was undertaking would be something that would be replicated on many of his future films – and directors would find an actor fuelled with ideas and a desire to add creative input.

Indeed, Wright remembered, 'Russell's the rudest actor I've ever met. He's also the most committed. So if he wants to abuse me and then give me the most sensational take of all time, I don't care.'

Russell took umbrage at that comment, blasting, 'I made a movie with him called *Romper Stomper*, the shoot of which was 28 days. I've known Wright for eight weeks of my life, in 1991, OK? So he's got no right to be giving quotes based on that.'

Whatever people thought about his processes, it was clear Russell was having a ball wrestling with a character that had some meat to him. 'It was an amazing experience. From the day we lost our hair it was almost like an avalanche. A film is like a train: if you don't get on and commit yourself to that journey you've got nothing. And you can't pull it over like a car. You stay on till the end. With *Romper Stomper* it was like, as soon as you got on the train it started to fall off the rails and over the cliff. Everything went crazy. And down the bottom was Geoff, still waving the remote control. Stupid analogy, actually.'

One aspect he didn't enjoy, however, was the explicit sex scenes, as he told *Vogue Men* in 1993. 'I really resent the fact that when you're doing a scene like that, the director will always take the female to one side and talk to her and look after her, whereas, if you're the bloke, you're left totally alone to cope with the situation. I also resent the notion that because you're a male you're trying to cop a free feel during a sex scene.

'And don't believe all that stuff about shooting those scenes on a closed set, because they're never really closed. There's usually a monitor in another room with the whole crew watching – that makes me furious. If I were the director in that situation, I would want them all sacked. Actors are not there to be pissed on.'

Russell thought it best to be a leader of his skinhead gang off-camera as much as on it. In a plan that he has since used on *Gladiator* and *Master and Commander* – films that again saw him be a leader of men – he would ensure that the hierarchy stayed the same even when the director said, 'Cut!' They would head out at night in full costume with their chests puffed out, goading locals with Nazi salutes.

'Those nine actors were my gang. They were all ranked. Everybody got a hat with a rank badge, and they all had different responsibilities in the group. Someone said, "Let's go down to the docks, to some working-class pub." And I said, "No, we're going to this very upwardly mobile hotel in South Yarra [in Melbourne]."

'Suddenly, in the middle of this, there are nine skinheads playing pool. In a working-class dockside pub it wouldn't have meant that much, but in that environment you get a quick appraisal for how much fear you can create in other people.

'I was very worried about what I was getting into when I arrived to do *Romper Stomper*. The gang situation is a volatile thing. Shave nine guys' heads, make them bond immediately, fire them to that level... To keep that under control takes a lot of effort and energy. That's not just me – that's Geoffrey and everybody else. Each guy was extremely brave, I reckon.

'The production company refused to let us physically train together, because they thought it was too dangerous and they didn't want to take the responsibility. So I organised it, unbeknown to them. I had an ex-skinhead, Greg, come in on a daily basis. He was a really nice fella. Isn't that funny? He'd gotten through it. Maybe he didn't need it so much any more.'

Russell was so determined to stay in wardrobe that he ended up being accosted by the police. 'One big night, nine of us got arrested. And we're not doing anything in particular, we're not hanging out in skinhead hangouts, we're just going to regular pubs. However, we don't have any hair, and we've got serious 16-hole fucking Doc Martens with white laces, which signify to the police "white supremacy". In an odd way, I was kind of weirdly comforted that these nine or ten blokes walking around together in Melbourne would immediately attract attention from the police.

'Two constables came out and grabbed me and said, "Who do you think you are?" and all that sort of stuff.

'I said, "Mate, I'll tell you exactly who we are – we're

a group of actors, and we're doing a movie where we're playing neo-Nazi skinheads."

'And this sergeant of police in South Melbourne says, "Is that right? Right. Well I hope you're a method actor, son, because you're really going to enjoy this. Put him in the fucking cell." At the time, I was really kind of angry, but over time you cannot help but laugh at that. That's funny as hell.'

It was one of several times that Russell was arrested during the shoot because of what he wore. Hando was also a character he would find hard to shake off, with Wright admitting that the actor went all out during a scene near the end where he attacks a woman. 'He's actually attacking her. It's hard to restrain Russell. If it's in the script and he hits someone, he kinda hits them. He doesn't bluff.'

Russell conceded, 'The best day I had playing the character was the last day of filming when I got the make-up off, got in my car and drove away from the set. I no longer had to think like him or read that crap they read or sit in my room listening to Wagner while watching *Triumph of the Will*. That was enough punishment for anyone. I was getting really sort of depressed about it. Towards the end I thought: "Jesus Christ, what am I doing here?"'

Not surprisingly, the press had a field day with the movie's subject matter – leaving Russell to exclaim, '[The] tabloid – bloody reactionary press. One thing the film does is make an audience examine their own bigotries. That's important, especially in this country where the middle-class broom sweeps problems under the carpet.'

Several journalists were unhappy with the film, accusing it of being sympathetic to Nazi skinheads. One journalist in particular, film critic David Stratton, called for the negative to be burned.

'Look, I've got respect for Dave Stratton, but he's from another generation. His reaction says to me that it's a very powerful film. I wouldn't want to offend him. I just wish he could distinguish in his own mind the difference between the ideology in the film and the ideology behind it.'

A denouncement from the mayor of Fitzroy in Melbourne only added to the film's notoriety – something that only pushed it further into cinemagoers' minds.

One of Russell's former band members, Raymond Eade, remembers, 'There was this guy who used to hate Russell, thought Russell was a little smartass prick. And he said to me, "Gee, I saw your mate Russell today in his movie *Romper Stomper* and he's really good." Russell was shit for this guy, but he was very impressed.'

There was tragedy for Russell, however, when his co-star Daniel Pollock, who he also starred with in *Proof*, died in 1992 after throwing himself in front of a train. The actor was addicted to heroin, but Russell insisted that it had never hindered him during filming. 'Sure, he had this addiction and it made it very hard for Daniel to keep focus, but it's not as if he was being propped up with a stick. He was the only guy who could keep up with me in sit-ups during training.

'I'm very sad Daniel's not around any more to see the film's success because he needed some sort of affirmation of his talent. But I don't see his death as suicide; I see it as an accident. Daniel was very accident-prone.'

Russell, who would later write a song entitled 'The Night That Davey Hit the Train', added, 'I was extremely angry about this [death] for a long time and I found it hard to talk about it without being vitriolic.'

For Wright, his experience working with Russell would last a lifetime. He didn't so much revel in working with Russell, but more survive it. But he did so with so many memories of someone who believes he will be remembered for years. 'You should never underestimate Russell,' he said. 'Russell may be a bull terrier but he's a very cunning one. There's most definitely a method to his madness as well as a madness to his method.

'Many American actors these days fail to work hard and are more concerned with star treatment on set. Therefore, Russell may continue to outshine them for quite some time and will remain the first choice of any A-list director wishing to make "the film of the year". He makes many of the Yankee leading men look like the under-skilled and over-precious wimps they truly are... I don't think that anyone who worked hard and had a commitment to the end result ever had an enduringly unpleasant time with Russell Crowe. Is this symptomatic of the perfectionist? I suppose, but God – look at the result in career rewards.'

CHAPTER EIGHT

RUSSELL SADDLES UP

'He has the gravity and masculinity that are disappearing from leading men.'

– Australian producer Al Clark

Romper Stomper was hailed as 'the most important Australian Film of The Year' in the *Sunday Morning Herald* – and Russell was fast becoming one of Australia's most important young actors.

'After *Romper Stomper*, I was immediately offered half a dozen roles with shaven heads and tattoos. I threw the scripts in the garbage. I hate typecasting. Repetition gets really bad for your head,' he told *That's Life* magazine.

It was clear he was fulfilling his potential but he wasn't ready for Hollywood just yet. His next film was *Hammers Over the Anvil*, a coming-of-the-age drama about a young boy struck by polio. The boy becomes obsessed with horseman East Driscoll (Russell) – a popular figure in the town who gets embroiled in a passionate love affair with the English wife (Charlotte Rampling) of a wealthy landowner.

It was based on a short story by Alan Marshall, and the film's producer Peter Harvey Wright had gone to see the author in 1982 in a bid to get the movie made. He said of their discussion, 'I was aware of treading carefully – just a little uncertain of how Alan would respond to some of my suggestions. When you are inspired by a writer and looking to transform their work to the screen, you have a strong desire to be absolutely faithful – to both the writer and the work – yet at the same time fulfil your own requirements.

'Then he leaned over to me and said most earnestly and with absolute resolution, "You know, you must remember that you are taking these words and these stories and you are setting them in another medium, another medium altogether. I used the medium and the form that I had at my disposal to gain the fullest effect that I could when I wrote those words, and you must feel free to do the same. Don't worry about my words."'

The film's director, Ann Turner, said about Russell, 'Russell was so right for the role – charismatic, earthy and extremely sensual. He's an amazing horseman and brings a great sense of power to the character.'

Hammers Over the Anvil would give Russell the chance to play a dashing leading man while reacquainting himself with horse riding – something he hadn't done in years.

The Silver Brumby's horse-riding consultant, Buddy Tyson, would later say to Russell, 'You're not an actor, you're a horseman.'

Every Sunday on his day off from filming *Romper Stomper,* Russell would head over from Melbourne to Mansfield to be trained in how to tackle the 16.2 thoroughbred stallion by experts Bill Willoughby and Gerald Egan. In the film's production notes, he said, 'The first time I cantered the horse up a hill I was addicted – the adrenaline rush was extraordinary as the speed and rhythm of the horse's body took control. We're talking one big racehorse with his own ideas of what he wanted to do, so it had to become a marriage of wills just to survive.'

He certainly threw himself into the role and made sure it would look believable on screen. He could be shooting up to 12 hours per day on horseback and he wanted to make sure that it was always him rather than a stuntman wherever possible. This would result in Russell falling off the horse several times during filming, earning him a few scratches and cuts and a severely bruised backside.

Talking about working with Russell, Rampling said, 'I found that he had a combination of being very outdoors and physical in one sense, but that he also had a very interesting sensitivity which would work beautifully with the role of East.'

The actress, who was 20 years his senior, added that he had 'a wild sense of humour'.

He would return the compliment, adding, 'She has a virtually perfect technical base, a big heart and a wonderful magic in her eyes. What you'll see on the screen is as close to falling in love as possible – the trick is getting out of it again.'

Despite the fact that the film would later be more known for its first scene, which sees Russell Crowe riding nude through a lake – the film's producer Ben Gannon was convinced at the time that *Hammers Over the Anvil* would confirm for good that his young actor was a rising talent. 'Russell is without a doubt the bright new male star on the horizon. He's passionate about his work and handles the complexities of the character's relationships superbly,' he said.

Despite fears of being typecast as 'that horse-opera' actor, Russell next agreed to work on *The Silver Brumby* – an adaptation of the classic book that has enthralled Australian children since it was published in the late 1950s.

Russell would play The Man – a loner who set outs to tame a wild horse. It was a script he had initially left untouched for weeks, but as soon as he read it he realised why the story was so cherished. 'I felt like I was seven years old and I had been transported on this magical journey. I had to do the film.'

There was one sticking point, however. In the film, his one companion is his loyal canine. He wanted the dog, an Australian shepherd dog named Coolie, to be with him at all times, to make their screen relationship believable. It was a request that was met with stern dismissal from the animal's trainer, Evanne Chesson.

'She looked at me and said, "Listen, I've worked in the Australian film business for 30 years and I've never met an actor yet that I'd allow even to wipe my dog's behind let alone live with him. So just forget it. I'll be bringing the dog to work, you'll get the dog at work, and I'll be taking the dog home. You got me?"'

The dog was at Russell's home within a week.

'She tuned into the fact that I was someone who genuinely did love animals, and things were fine. The dog went everywhere I did for the whole film. He was a beautiful dog. It was really quite upsetting emotionally to have to leave him at the end of shooting. I know that sounds quite stupid, but that's the way it was.'

Director John Tatoulis said about working with the actor, 'He was very passionate and could get very angst-ridden and fiery at times, but then it was always about the work. I don't mind a bit of emotion if it's in the cause of doing your best. Russell was always trying to do the best performances he could.'

Russell, he said, was terrific to work with. 'It was great to see how he related to the horses. One of the things I enjoyed about working with Russell in particular was that he really did live his character once he put on his costume. He really wanted to be part of that mountain environment and he truly got into it.

'And watching that process and watching him get into character and be at one with the mountains, be at one with the horses, was very interesting. At the same time he was working with a lot of the local riders, lots of local high countrymen. They felt it odd that Russell wouldn't take off his costume – that he wanted to be more of a high countryman than they were – but after a little while they really did embrace him as well. It was an interesting process.

As with *Love in Limbo*, the role stands out from the later intense roles that litter Russell's filmography, but it is one that he is proud of. 'It was a kids' film made for pony club girls aged between eight and 12, and it was a great part of Oz history to document it on film. It's a magical story and I'd love some 25-year-old to come up to me one day and say, "I saw you in that film when I was a kid."'

In a 1997 interview, he added, 'After *Romper Stomper*, I did this kids' film called *The Silver Brumby*, because I thought, "I gotta do one for my niece." I spent three or four months in the mountains in Victoria riding a horse, rounding up cattle, and cooking steaks at five o'clock in the morning in this little hut I was living in. I had maybe half a dozen lines of dialogue. It wasn't like making a film – it was like experiencing a totally different lifestyle.'

It's not a film that his own kids ended up loving, however. 'I went to put on a movie for my kids because my son Charlie said, "Everybody tells me you make movies, but I've never seen any". And I thought, "OK, what's the most innocuous one I've done? Oh, *Mystery, Alaska*, about this ice hockey guy." I put it on and in my first scene I've got two other sons who are not my sons.

'Charlie starts laughing and I said, "Oh, OK. I'll turn this one off." The only film they've seen that I've done is *The Silver Brumby*. It's a kids' film and Charlie's very confused by it because I'm galloping around on horseback chasing a horse, but when he's with me on the farm, I just call and the horse comes. So it's like, "Why are you doing all that? Why don't you just call?"

'I showed him 30 seconds of *Master and Commander*. It just happened to be the storm sequence, when I'm hanging off the side of the boat in the waves. I said, "What do you think of that?" and he goes, "Way too scary, Daddy."'

As Russell was becoming more and more known in Australia, he began to think about the next step. 'Very quickly in Australia I got all the recognition that there is to get there, in terms of awards and stuff. And so suddenly I had to look overseas and look at expanding where I was going to work. In Australia, once you get that level of recognition, you're supposed to sit down for ten years and they'll re-discover you in your forties, you know? But I wasn't satisfied with that because I was only just starting to work.'

America would be calling, and it would be one of their biggest female stars who was making that call to get

Russell into her movie. But that was before he found out the hard way that being a big fish in a small pond didn't mean a thing in Hollywood.

CHAPTER NINE

CROW FLIES TO HOLLYWOOD

'It's very easy for me to have friction with Americans because I'm very positive about what I want to do.'

– Russell Crowe

Russell arrived in L.A. determined to make his mark on Hollywood. Not that he had any doubts this would happen. In 1992, he had met up with Hollywood agent George Freeman from the world-famous International Creative Management (ICM) agency.

'I asked him a couple of questions,' Russell said. 'They were questions other people had given me bullshit answers to, really personal questions. He looked me straight in the eye when he answered and I knew he was telling me the truth.

'You get accused of being arrogant by some people because I seem to – in some people's viewpoints – expect success. But it doesn't surprise me when it comes, because I know how much work I put into it.'

His roles had been diverse enough to give him

confidence in his talents, but it was *Romper Stomper* that stood out on his CV. And so he did what many other international actors do when they head to L.A. in a bid to find success there: they meet an endless number of people, press flesh with names they forget almost immediately and smile. A lot.

That was something which Russell did, although he disliked the hangers-on that surrounded the industry. But the final straw came when he attended a party held in his honour by ICM. 'It was a very short party,' Russell said. 'I split. Hollywood parties are not my vibe. I'm into the more traditional Australian party: beer in a bathtub and you have a good sing.'

He would make the trip from Australia to L.A. more than a dozen times – mostly funded from his own pocket – and each time he would return disappointed. In a town where nearly everyone is a frustrated actor longing for his chance, it was hard to stand out. He was asked to play the game, but that was something he had very little time for.

A role in the Canadian World War II romantic drama *For the Moment* was a step in the right direction. It tells the story of a romance between Australian fighter pilot Lachlan (Russell) and his friend's sister Kate (Sara McMillan). It received generally positive reviews, with most of the praise centred on Russell as the poetry-spouting army man.

'Crowe is excellent as Lachlan, proving that even years before be became a box-office sensation he could anchor a film. His Lachlan could easily have been a mere stock character, the cocky young flier who learns some tough lessons about life and love (*Top Gun*, anyone?), but Crowe creates a character more complex, believable and thoughtful, a man we quickly grow to care about,' said *DVD Review*, while *Reel Views* said that Russell was 'far superior to anyone else in the cast'.

His mother also cites it as one of her favourites of her son's movies.

While Russell's career in Hollywood wasn't progressing as fast as he would have liked, it didn't meant that he would cut corners in the acting stakes. He took the role of Lachlan as seriously as any of his previous parts.

The film's location manager, Dave Mahoney, remembered, 'He was very hard on himself, and maybe that's why he's so good. From what I saw, as far as his temperament on set, I've seen a lot worse, that's for sure. And from a lot less gifted. He was good, he knew he was good, and he expected good things from himself.'

Director Aaron Kim Johnston added, 'He's quite a perfectionist – he's very professional. He approaches his craft and work with great intensity and preparation and a sense of perfectionism that is consummate. That's why he is wherc he is.

'I think he likes to be a maverick. It's certainly part of his nature and the other part of it is that he likes to be a little bit of a disturber. I think he's going to cut some of the bullshit out of things. If Russell's involved, chances are it'll be a little less processed. And that's a good thing for audiences.'

However, Russell was despondent about his situation, often phoning his girlfriend Danielle nearly in tears. Ironically, it would be an Australian film rather than an American one that would get his hunger back. It was a script that Russell loved immediately and was one that would ruffle the feathers of fans who had begun to see him as a typical macho Australian heterosexual male.

'People are going to go spare when they hear I'm playing a homosexual football player, and they already have. They've been just stunned. But the way I see it is that it's one hell of a challenge.'

The Sum of Us told the story of Jeff (Russell), a gay rugby player whose father helps his son find Mr Right. It was a role he jumped at, not caring that it sent him back to Australia to make it. He had rejected several Australian film roles at the time but *The Sum of Us* was too good to turn down. He was quick to point out that he wasn't bothered about playing a gay character.

'There are many questions I would ask a character – for instance, "Do you believe in the death penalty?" – before I ever got round to "What's your sexuality?" I think other factors are more important in terms of human relationships and the way society operates than what someone's sexuality is. Sexual orientation is not something that people necessarily choose; it's just who they are.'

John Polson would play his lover in the film, and the pair would head to gay nightclubs in Sydney, where Russell observed, 'I got right inside the gay community without making it known, and I discovered for the most part they're people looking for pretty much exactly the same thing as heterosexuals.'

While he was happy to head to gay spots, he wasn't keen on researching man-on-man kissing with Polson. 'I was waiting around when John came over and said, "Do you want to practise kissing?" I looked at him and said, "John, are you sick?" He said, "Well, I've never kissed a man before." And I said, "Well, neither have I. But how do you think it would be if I went up to Sharon Stone before a love scene and said, 'Hey Shaz, how do you feel about practising kissing?'" I don't think so.'

It may have been an unusual request but for someone who prides himself on his dedication for research – 'If you're gonna be a pirate, wear a patch' – Russell was somewhat defensive about it. Ironically, this perceived reluctance could be what makes *The Sum of Us* stand out. It's impossible to know what other actors would have done with the character, but where some would add fey mannerisms to a gay character – which was seen in many films at the time – Russell imbued Jeff with a vein of laddish masculinity. The only thing that was different about Jeff from the other guys in the pub was his sexuality.

He explained, 'It says, "OK, now look, he plays football,

he's a plumber, he's a nice bloke, he loves his dad, he's a very loyal son. He's got all these aspects – he's just got a difference in sexuality." Now do you want to condemn him, do you want to vilify him, or do you want to understand that in the world there is a whole range of things going on and the banging of podiums and all the screaming and yelling should be done towards things that are much more important than sexuality?

'I think *The Sum of Us* may have a central character at that particular point but it does go into other aspects of gay life and gay lifestyles. I don't think that anybody ever intended that this was the absolute bible for how to live a gay lifestyle – this is just one particular guy.

'The way I see Jeff's "normality" is that you don't really know [that he's gay], and all the traditional things of masculinity are having a new light shined on them. That's what I think it's about.'

The film also managed to avoid the usual clichés that adorn gay dramas – by having the father (played by Jack Thompson) approve of his son's sexuality. The only thing that hurts him is seeing his son not find the happiness he deserves.

To be fair to Russell, a reluctance to kiss his co-star in rehearsals didn't translate on screen. He goes all out in the intimate love scene, which would of course receive some media attention from outraged columnists.

He would say when the film opened in 1994 that he hoped the film would tackle people's perception of homosexuality. 'If we can put a tenth of what we did for putting racism on the table for conversation with *Romper Stomper*, then I'll be ecstatic.'

Actually, the film's release would lead to suggestions and whispers that Russell was himself homosexual. Spencer remembers overhearing in a bar two people talking about a friend's performance in the film – with one casually remarking that he knew Russell's boyfriend. However, it turned out that this mystery pal happened to be a gay friend whom Russell had consulted about where the best gay bars were in a bid to get into character.

Russell had already met his on-screen father while he roamed the Australian TV sets as a youngster. 'Jack was the star of the TV show I did when I was six years old. Then, 23 years later, I got to play his son. It was one of those great cosmic circles that this industry affords you every now and then. In many respects, Jack was my father in terms of screen performance,' he said in 1997.

The pair's chemistry is immediate in the film, and it seems to have translated off-camera. Indeed, Thompson hailed his 'wonderful friend', saying, 'I admire his success, and that's not such a silly thing to say either. I admire his success, because his success implies that an actor of that quality, of that heart, of that focus, of that sort of uncompromising search for quality, is vindicated and seriously vindicated. And that you can be a really good actor, and a successful movie star ... I admire that enormously. I admire him as an actor, because he's astute, he's studied, and he's instinctive at the same time, and that produces a very fine performance and makes him a delight to work with.

'Acting is, of course, totally interactive, and it depends on the quality of the other person on the other side of the net, to extend the tennis metaphor. And if the person on the other side of the net is really good, and you're kind of good yourself, you will see some fantastic tennis. I think some of the scenes in *The Sum of Us* between Russell and I are some of the best acting in my 30-year career, without a doubt.'

A minor hit in Australia, the movie garnered positive reviews, with *The San Francisco Chronicle* raving, '*The Sum of Us* isn't exactly cutting-edge, but it takes a few chances (or what might be perceived as chances by an American viewing audience). Jeff's homosexuality is a complete non-issue. There's nothing political or tragic in his situation. In fact, he and the other characters frequently joke about it.'

And:

'Thompson brings skill, humor and conviction to *The Sum of Us,* as does Crowe, who at 28 looks primed for stardom.'

Despite the film's success, Russell still had an eye on Hollywood – and at this point it finally come calling. And it was one of their biggest female stars who was on the line.

CHAPTER TEN

RUSSELL AND THE WILD WEST

'I don't think the Americans really understood him at first. They put him in a lot of stupid films. I think he bullied a lot of American directors. I think they were frightened of him.'

– Geoffrey Wright

It was an early morning when Russell woke up, his head thumping from the night before and his mind as empty as his pockets. It only took him a brief moment, though, to piece back together what had happened. Frustrated at countless visits to Los Angeles with very little to show for it, he had headed out of Los Angeles on a whim on a road trip to Las Vegas. Cue much drinking and a shrinking bank balance. Unknown to him, however, he was being proposed for a role in a Hollywood blockbuster – and it was the film's leading lady who was desperate to have Russell in *The Quick and the Dead*.

Sharon Stone was big news at the time. After a series of underwhelming roles throughout her early acting career, she was propelled into the limelight after her breakthrough performance in *Basic Instinct*. The equally erotic *Sliver*'s box office success proved that she wasn't just a flash in the pan. Now she wanted to produce.

A Western starring Stone as the heroine may have seemed a somewhat risky choice, but her stock had never been higher. Gene Hackman was drafted in to play the mayor of Redemption – a corrupt man who rules the town with a ruthless fist. His annual shooting contest, which weeds out the opposition, attracts a group of misfit gunslingers including The Kid (Leonardo DiCaprio) and Ellen (Stone). She arrives in town to plot her revenge against the mayor for a past injustice.

If a female lead in a genre that hadn't done too well at the box office of late was risky, so were her choices of director and leading man. Despite a shortlist of potential directors lined up, Stone only had one name in mind – Sam Raimi.

Raimi would go on to become a hugely successful director with the *Spider-Man* films and win critical acclaim with the thriller *A Simple Plan*, but at that time he was best known for directing the cult horror *Evil Dead* series. He was a bold choice – albeit one who was already successful thanks to his trademark highly stylised visuals and inventive camera shots. 'He was the only one who could make this film,' she said. 'He's a true visionary and I knew he could turn *The Quick and the Dead* into his own kind of film. Sam is his own genre. This isn't a Western; it's a Sam Raimi film.'

While the studio bosses agreed on Raimi and were delighted to get someone of Hackman's stature, they were less keen on Stone's choice to play Bud Cort, the former gunslinger turned preacher. He was a heroic character – a really iconic gunslinger Hollywood archetype. The studio were convinced they could get a big and recognisable name for the part, so they were less than pleased to see that Stone and Raimi wanted Russell Crowe.

Raimi had seen Russell in *Romper Stomper* and was hugely impressed with what he saw, as was Stone when Raimi showed her the film. 'We must meet him,' she told her director.

'When I saw *Romper Stomper*, I thought Russell was not only charismatic, attractive and talented but also fearless. And I find fearlessness very attractive. I was convinced that I wouldn't scare him,' she said.

Certainly, Russell was not someone who would ever feel overshadowed by other actors. But he and Stone share very similar traits. They are both feisty, strong-willed and talented individuals who believe they have come through to be movie stars through hard work and perseverance.

Stone certainly saw something of herself in Russell – someone who wouldn't say what the other wanted to hear. He was forthright and opinionated. On their first meeting, after hearing her talk about the merits of a pre-nuptial, he said, 'If you're going to have a pre-nuptial agreement, isn't there something wrong with the person you've selected for your marriage partner for life?'

It was a remark that pleased her – and with that, coupled with their earlier meeting that day which saw him as far removed from his *Romper Stomper* character as he could be, she knew she had her leading man. 'He wasn't this cold, isolated tough guy,' she recalled. 'He was a funny, vulnerable goofball, with this beautiful head of hair and beautiful blue eyes. I thought, "Wow, this guy's going to be a movie star."'

She would also say later, 'Russell Crowe is the sexiest actor working in movies today.'

However, the studio bosses wanted Irish actor Liam Neeson for the role of Cort. And with Raimi having previous working experience with Neeson on the superhero tale *Darkman*, it looked as though Russell would lose out. He was also hampered by the fact that he was contracted to work on *The Sum of Us*, and if he were to get the part it would mean filming would have to be pushed back until he had finished work on that.

'Basically the studio said to her, "We don't know who's going to play the role but it's not going to be that guy, some unknown fella from Australia." And she just went, "Oh really?"'

During his screen test, he found out exactly what pressures Stone was facing in her bid to cast him in the film. 'An executive at TriStar rang Sharon in the middle of my screen test and demanded that she come off the soundstage and take the call,' he told *Vanity Fair*. 'So she said, "Come with me." We went into this room, and she put him on speaker phone. And he just spewed this fucking bile about, "You may be the producer, but you're stepping over the line, and I'm gonna get a great actor for the role, and I can tell you one thing – it won't be some fucking Australian with dubious credits." When he rang off, she said, "I just wanted you to know what I'm up against."'

The constant battles would take their toll on Stone. 'By the time we were ready to make the movie, I didn't want to make it. I was worn out. We did all the fighting before we got here.'

As a result, the environment wasn't exactly a happy one – and it was different from other sets that Russell had worked on. 'I had never been on a set or stage show surrounded by people with so much fear,' he told the *Sunday Times*. 'They feared for their jobs because it has become traditional that the director fires some of the crew in the first couple of weeks. That is not how you should deal with creative people. It was a strange environment, and I felt very much like the meat in the sandwich between Gene Hackman and Sharon Stone, plus a whole bunch of actors who had never heard of me and didn't know what the hell I was doing there.'

While Russell enjoyed working with Raimi – who would later call him a gentleman – and Stone, he had a less than cordial relationship with Hackman. 'Here's this young Australian guy coming in to play what, on paper, is the third lead in a $35 million film and nobody's heard of him except for Sharon. So I wouldn't say it was easy for any of these guys to accept that they should give over any kind of respect or consideration at all.'

Another reason for Hackman's reported indifference towards Russell could be attributed to Crowe making light of his veteran co-star's hairstyle. 'I think I made a joke about the permed hair,' he revealed.

Unfazed, Russell also said that it wasn't a bad thing that the pair weren't the best of friends, considering they play sworn enemies in the film.

Talking about Russell, Raimi admitted, 'He's a tough bastard to get along with. The problem with working with Russell is that he always has a good idea. And he has no tact! He tells you. Sometimes he stood the whole scene on its head. It's not easy by a long chalk to work with Russell. But it's exciting and it pays off dramatically.'

Russell has defended his process, saying, 'People accuse me of being arrogant all the time. I'm not arrogant, I'm focused. I don't make demands. I don't tell you how it should be. I'll give you fucking options, and it's up to you to select or throw 'em away. That should be the headline: If you're insecure, don't fucking call.'

An extra on the set of the film, who only wanted to be identified as a citizen of Redemption, said, 'Russell Crowe was an interesting character. His thick Australian accent virtually disappeared when he was on camera but would instantly return when they stopped rolling.

'He was a bit more temperamental than the others – although not excessively so – but I believe that was because he was very dedicated and worked very hard.

'Case in point: he spent many hours learning the art of gunslinging. Those twirling tricks he does in Kid Fee's gun shop were actually done by him. He got very good at it and often practised between takes.

'We spent 16 hours in the saloon "hanging him" during one very long night. He worked harder that night than anyone, since he had to be at the brink of strangulation most of the time. He was wearing a safety harness with a hidden wire, but he still had to keep the rope tight against his neck, while on tiptoes, through the shooting of that entire scene. I have a lot of respect for him.'

During filming Russell struck up a relationship with a young actor by the name of Leonardo DiCaprio, who recalled of their time together: 'I was 18 at the time... I had done *Gilbert Grape* and Russell had done *Romper Stomper*. We were both hand-plucked to do this big-budget film. We were both very bright-eyed and bushy-tailed.'

The pair would work together again on 2008's *Body of Lies*, but at that moment, they were just newbies on the Hollywood scene. 'There was a difference in our ages but we were both in the same sort of position,' said Russell.

'The people "above us" in the cast were Gene Hackman and Sharon Stone, and everyone "below us" were all these really famous character actors like Keith David and cats like that, and they're looking at the two of us going, "Who are these guys?" And that naturally put us together.'

Citizen of Redemption remembered of DiCaprio: 'He seemed to take his role less seriously than the others. The extras even helped with his lines on several occasions.

'Leo often bummed cigarettes from the extras, including several from me. I went to see *Titanic* right after it was released. In that film, at one point Leo goes up to someone and asks if he can bum a smoke. I was the only one in the crowded theatre who burst out laughing aloud at this line. Leo still owes me some smokes.'

Russell had a lot of time for his leading lady – at first. She not only represented for him someone who went out of her way to give a young actor a break in Hollywood, but he admired her for her professionalism at all times. The dual strain of producer and star was taking a toll on her but still she would arrive on set on time and joke with the cast and crew.

The pair spent Christmas Day at the Salvation Army at Stone's request after hearing that Russell was going to spend the day alone. 'So we spend Christmas morning serving food at the Salvation Army. And from there we went to a home for battered children,' recalled Russell. 'We just played with the kids, gave them presents. You look into the eyes of a woman like that, what she could be doing on Christmas Day, and you realise what she is doing on Christmas Day and she is still in that single percentage of actresses who know what glamour is and what being a movie star is all about. I'm a big supporter of hers. I think she's a great person.'

However, he would also say in another interview, 'She was instrumental in me getting my first American job. Absolutely, without her support, it would not have happened. At the same time, however, was it really about me or her wanting to flex her producerial muscles? I don't want to sound ungallant about the situation. But I didn't find that in working with her, that we clicked on any other level.'

It was a bittersweet Hollywood debut, and done for low pay. Russell returned to Australia in debt and smarting from comments by some Australian actors who said they would never work for so little money. 'What are you doing now?' he would retort.

'And it's something like public theatre in New South Wales. They don't realise it took two years out of my life to get that role, for which I got no money. Nothing you want to do is ever easy.

'I got paid less than anybody who was an extra for the whole film. Finally, the only thing between Sharon getting me in the movie and me doing it was money.

'She pushed so many studio requisites out of the way in order to have me in the movie, based on the fact she thought I was good. It was like, well, there's no consideration there. Forget about money. It's not about that, I'm coming for the work.'

Just as Stone had had with *The Quick and the Dead*, director Brett Leonard faced a difficult task trying to get studio approval for Russell to be in his sci-fi movie *Virtuosity*. Like Raimi and Stone, Leonard had been hugely impressed by Russell's work on *Romper Stomper*, and even sent the actor a letter urging him to join his cast.

Russell remembered, 'It took him seven months to convince the studio that I should play the role. He had two or three meetings a week where they would put a sheet in front of him with five blank spaces on it and say, "Just write your top five." He would write my name five times and hand it back to them.'

The studio were unsure, but after seeing a screen test with him and the main star Denzel Washington, they reluctantly agreed. Not that his audition went perfectly – he accidentally spat in the face of Washington. 'Now I'm horrified,' Russell recalled. 'I'm thinking, "Great, I just (messed) this up." But Denzel, he's such a professional – such a stand-up guy, he just keeps going like nothing happened.

'[He] turns back to me and says, "I love the taste of saliva in the morning."'

The film stars Washington as a former cop turned convict, who will be granted a full pardon if he can stop a virtual-reality serial killer – in a police training program that incorporates some of the world's most notorious serial killers. Sid 6.7 (Sadistic. Intelligent. Dangerous) was played by Russell in fine devilish form.

Talking about his character, Russell said, 'It's pretty far out. As is revealed in the movie, Sid is totally interactive so he's just playing with what he's got. He's come out of the machine, he's looked around, he's examined humanity in the one half of the millisecond it takes him to work it out, and he realises that human beings couldn't possibly go around doing what they do if they didn't want to die. He's just trying to help them out. He's a very generous guy!'

Denzel said about his co-star, 'Russell is wild. He's very intense, a very excellent actor. An actor who really comes in prepared but at the same time likes to have a good laugh.'

The film's producer, Garry Lucchesi, raved, 'Russell is absolutely fantastic. He's a rock 'n' roller. He's a movie star. So often you see stereotypical villains, and that was one thing we really did not want Sid cast as.

'I've loved the idea of casting leading men to play villains as opposed to character actors, and I think Russell is a true leading man and is going to be a great star. Ultimately the movie became quite elevated by having an Academy Award-winning actor like Denzel and a really talented actor like Russell.'

This was the film where Russell believed he was finally there as an actor. 'I knew when I was doing *Virtuosity*, when I was working opposite Denzel, that I had the things that I needed and I could communicate the things that I had constructed intellectually and physically.' In fact most reviews would claim that it was Russell's performance that lingered most.

After his scene-stealing performance in *Virtuosity*, he was soon being offered more roles. The underwhelming kidnap thriller *No Way Back* was first, followed by romantic comedy *Rough Magic* alongside Bridget Fonda. The latter, a spiritual tale based on the novel *Miss Shumway Waves a Wand* by James Hadley Chase, tells the story of a world-weary reporter falling in love with a magician's assistant.

Russell admitted he was keen to play a parody of film noir tough guys, as he put it. 'When I first read the script, I loved its wit and pace,' he said. 'It's about a lot of different things. It's about, in a broad sense, the spirituality and magic we all contain and whether or not you can tap into it and whether you can open up enough to believe in it.'

But it wasn't a hit at the box office nor was it a favourite with the critics, although the esteemed film critic Roger Ebert noted: 'Russell Crowe is steady in the Mitchum role, as a guy hired to do a job who falls in love with the dame.'

Russell next went on to star in the comedy-drama *Breaking Up* – a quirky look at a couple's on-off relationship. About *Breaking Up*, he said, 'Well, what

I've tried to do since being invited to make movies in America is not just take safer large-studio and budget options. I've tried to make smaller films as well as the larger ones, because I'd like to look at the American film industry from many different levels and not just from the big one.

'*Breaking Up* had a small budget and it was a very complex script in terms of what it asked from performance. Mainly, it was a series of really late nights – just trying to cram those lines into my brain, you know? Because of that low budget there was no real rehearsal period. It was like, "Here's the script" and you're off. At the time we made it I was coming off *Virtuosity* with Denzel Washington, which was a very strange filmmaking experience in itself because of all the blue-screen work involved. I mean, you're in this blank room grabbing stuff out of the air that doesn't exist, and then three or four months later you've got a rose in your hand or you're playing the piano or something like that.

'So *Breaking Up* was about getting down and doing something a little bit more basic and real and performer-aligned. It was a really fast shoot, something like 28 days, really intense. Part of the shoot was in New York City, and we were there at the same time as the Pope and the chess championship and the president, you know? I mean, there's bad enough traffic as it is, but when you bring all those clowns in ... it was pretty rough.'

Salma Hayek would say of her time working with

Russell – who she would describe as one of the two best actors she's ever worked with – 'He's a little difficult. But we ended up bonding because we both fell in love with the film.

'It was a tough shoot. We were overworking, we were gong crazy and you don't want to see Russell Crowe in these circumstances.'

She recalled one incident that found them turning up for filming and finding a makeshift dressing room – essentially a towel lying on the floor. Because Russell had arrived first, she asked, 'Did you throw a fit already?'

'He said, "Yes" and I went, "OK then, I won't say anything." Because I knew he must have killed them.'

Talking about his time making his first Hollywood movies, Russell said, 'I was always feted and patted on the back in those L.A. meetings. You think you're loved and respected, but that is bollocks. The job is not real until you are in front of the camera, doing it.'

And he would be certainly be doing it in his next film. While he felt the backslaps weren't sincere, it was also probably down to Russell's own assertion that he hadn't earned them. Luckily, he was to land a part that made Hollywood sit up and take notice.

CHAPTER ELEVEN

L.A. CONFIDENTIAL

'The other actor's in his corner and somebody rings a bell and you come out and do your business.'

– Russell Crowe

Based on the 1990 novel by esteemed crime fiction writer James Ellroy, *L.A. Confidential* tells the story of a group of Los Angeles policemen in the 1950s against the backdrop of police corruption and Hollywood sleaze.

Producer Curtis Hanson said that the reason for doing the film was his love of Ellroy's characters. 'What hooked me on them was that as I met them, one after the other, I didn't like them – but as I continued reading, I started to care about them.'

Screenwriter Brian Helgeland was such a fan of the book, and indeed Ellroy's L.A. quartet series, in which *L.A. Confidential* was the third part, that he not only lobbied hard for the job of writing the film but he worked on the script for two years with Hanson – and wrote seven drafts for free.

'Curtis had a doggedness about him,' Helgeland recalled. 'He would turn down other jobs. I would be doing drafts for free. Whenever there was a day when I didn't want to get up any more, Curtis tipped the bed and rolled me out on the floor.'

The task of tackling Ellroy's sprawling novel was a mammoth one, and not many, including the writer himself, were convinced that the book could be condensed into a film. But Helgeland managed it.

'They preserved the basic integrity of the book and its main theme ... Brian and Curtis took a work of fiction that had eight plotlines, reduced those to three, and retained the dramatic force of three men working out their destiny,' Ellroy said later.

In a 2009 interview with *Empire*, he added, 'It's the greatest thing that has happened in my career, in that I had nothing to do with it. I was given a world that sprang from my imagination, but a world I could have not imagined on my own.'

To convince studio bosses to take a chance on his film, Hanson put together a visual presentation that included postcards and pictures of L.A. in that time period (items that he had amassed all through his life). A picture of 'the famous shot of [Robert] Mitchum coming out of jail on his marijuana charge, where he looks incredibly handsome and buffed out' flirted with images of musicians, while other celebrities of the time filled out the other parts of the presentation.

'Always,' Hanson said, 'I emphasised that the period would be in the background, the characters and emotions in the foreground. And I said there would be something lurid and flashy and fun about it. Near the end I brought out a couple of old movie-star glamour things, including one of Veronica Lake, and said, "This is what we're not doing, except when Lynn Bracken is selling it to the suckers."

'Then I wrapped up with a couple of modern shots by Helmut Newton of sexy women today wearing retro-style clothes, to show why the guys in the audience would be going, "Yeah!"'

Producer Arnon Milchan was suitably impressed ('I see the movie in your eyes,' he told Hanson) and agreed to make the movie.

The two most important characters in the film are policemen Bud White and Ed Exley, both of whom were to be played by two relatively unknown Australian actors – Russell and Guy Pearce respectively. Like Russell, Pearce had been an actor on *Neighbours*.

Hanson knew straight away that Russell fitted the visual description of Bud White, and he was convinced that he could handle the dramatic side after seeing *Romper Stomper* – a performance that Hanson said he found 'repulsive and scary but captivating'. 'We flew him over here, I met with him, we talked about the character and I put him on tape doing a scene.' The tape shows a long-haired Russell Crowe acting out an intense scene from the start of the film.

Pearce had shot to fame playing a man in drag in *The Adventures of Priscilla Queen of the Desert*. 'Curtis hadn't seen *Priscilla* at the time I auditioned as Ed Exley,' the actor said. 'He decided not to, which was a good idea. He thought it might influence his judgment if he had a vivid impression of me running around in drag for two hours. It might have messed things up. I had met him only the day before I read.'

Russell and Pearce were hired because Hanson wanted audiences to go through the same feeling that he had while reading the book. 'You don't like any of these characters at first, but the deeper you get into their story, the more you begin to sympathise with them. I didn't want actors [that] audiences knew and already liked,' he said.

The decision to mould the film around Russell and Pearce was a brave one, and one that Arnon Milchan – one of the film's backers – worried about. 'Is this movie going to have any stars?' he is reported to have said after agreeing to cast the two actors.

'His backing me at the start about those two guys empowered me with every move I made from then on,' Hanson told the *Dallas Observer* in 1997. 'It put me in the unique position of going to Kim Basinger and Kevin Spacey and Danny DeVito and saying, "I'm making this movie that I love. We start shooting in three weeks. Do you want to be in it?"'

Hanson added, 'I have been a director-for-hire, and as

such you get what you can get and do the best you can. I have been lucky enough to have had a couple of commercial successes which empowered me and gave me some clout. In a sense, this was both a major studio film, which it needed to be because of the cost of making it [an estimated $50 million], and an independent movie. Miraculously, Warner Bros not only embraced my ideas but went along with this wacky casting.'

Hanson had wanted Basinger for the part in one of his earlier films, *The Hand that Rocks the Cradle*, but after she had made disparaging remarks about Disney after finishing *The Marrying Man*, there was no way the company was going to re-hire her for the thriller.

'Kim was the character to me,' Hanson said. 'What beauty today could project the glamour of Hollywood's Golden Age? Plus, what actress can play the role? I've always been a fan of Kim's and wanted to work with her in the past. I think she's the only one who could play this part.'

Before shooting began, Russell and Pearce were taken to Los Angeles for nearly two months to immerse them in the city; they also watched several film noirs from that period, including Robert Aldrich's excellent *Kiss Me Deadly*.

'Russell and I had bumped into each other back home but we hadn't worked together and weren't pals,' Pearce explained. 'I didn't test with him for *L.A. Confidential*. But coming on board so early gave us a funny advantage.

We developed a fairly strong friendship but also started to think of the whole thing as our show.

'Russell and I were going to what were called rehearsals, which consisted of us and Curtis and the screenwriter, Brian Helgeland, sitting around and discussing each scene. I had met Kevin [Spacey] at a party during that period and told him that I thought one of the roles, Pierce Patchett, would suit him admirably. And it would have, but now he's rather too important for such a small role.

'We turned up for rehearsals for one day and there was Kevin, about to read for Jack Vincennes, the third of the tarnished police heroes.'

Both lead actors found that the vintage films were more useful than working with modern-day policemen, with Pearce hating his time around one certain police officer because he was racist. They would work on the script each day with Hanson and Helgeland, going through each scene.

For Pearce, this was a chance to make a Hollywood movie of old, rather than the ones of late. He told the *Washington Post* in 1997, 'Most American movies are about some guy that's kind of living on the edge and saves the world and has the chick and does the gun stuff. And it's full of all those stupid one-liners that mean nothing. I want something a lot more than that. Have you seen *Face/Off*? I hate slagging off other movies but I thought it was rubbish. Banal chase scenes, trained shooters missing their targets...'

He added, 'This was much bigger than anything I've done, but I don't think this was considered to be a big-budget American film. We were such a close-knit group. Danny was wonderful. And Kim is just adorable.'

Russell would say about Guy, 'One of the best things about doing this movie was working with him. It was so great to have someone like him there to help me through. I mean, when the days were long and the thing feels like a real job, hard work, it was terrific to have someone there who was both a great actor and a great guy,' he told *Celluloid* in 1997.

'One of the things that we discussed when we first talked, when we knew we were going to do the job, was when we did actually come together as a team, it should be like two halves of a whole. These two guys should actually make up one decent cop.'

Talking about Spacey, he added, 'He's the most charming man. He's the Oscar Wilde of our time. I only had one moment with him in that film and it's a great source of regret. I love spending time with him. He's always very open and effusive. His interest in you is genuine.'

Talking about his character, Russell said, 'He's a racist. He's self-righteous. He's foul-mouthed. He's a son of a bitch. However, in the course of the movie, you get an indication as to why he's taken this attitude toward life. He doesn't realise just how much he's looking for love and affection and confirmation of his good points, buried as they may be. ... I think he is a good man – but he's very much a product of his environment and his job.'

Although Bud and Exley are central to the story, it's the city that is probably the main character of the film.

Hanson, who gave the film noir story a modern visual look, told the *Dallas Observer*, 'I also found myself thinking about the city. Ellroy gave me the opportunity to set a movie at a point in time when the whole dream of Los Angeles, from that apparently golden era of the 1920s and 1930s, was being bulldozed. The area was changing from this group of individual little communities to the megalopolis that the freeways created.

'The mood after World War II was very un-noirish. It was one of optimism and economic boom. And there were a lot of things starting here, new and exciting, that for better or worse are still very much with us today. The freeways, the whole idea of suburbia. Television, tabloid journalism. It's the period that I lived through as a child, and this seemed to be an opportunity to tell a story about these characters and that city all in one.'

The Formosa Café seen in the film was going to be torn down by Warner Bros because they owned the studios across the street and they wanted to build a car park. 'I'm one of the advisors on the L.A. Conservancy,' said Hanson. 'So I told them about the plans, they got on the case and prevented Warners from doing it.'

To prepare for the role, Russell said, 'I hired a flat that was very small. I could hardly even fit into the doorway of the bathroom but to me, every day doing that I felt like I was big. I was oversized for my environment, which was the mentality that Bud White was supposed to have.'

He also stopped drinking beer. 'One of the most painful things of the *L.A. Confidential* character I played was that the author, James Ellroy, kept telling me that Bud White didn't drink beer, but scotch. Now I can tell what's blended and what's single malt. But I haven't actually had any since the moment we finished shooting this movie, because it's disgusting.'

Russell is defensive about accusations that such acts are ultimately self-indulgent and don't add much to the acting process. 'I assure you it's not a silly game that I played during the shoot, to see if Ellroy will allow me a drink or not,' he said in an interview. 'That trait was an essential part of the guy, it was one of his defining traits. You can't drink beer when that act alters the character in such a fundamental way.'

He would continue, 'But that is something natural. Let's say that you more or less keep the character in your head. But don't think that I'm one of those crazy actors that answer in the character's voice when people talk to them on the street, or that during the shoot they insist on being called with the character's name, or that only dress in the movie's clothes and so on. No, nothing like that. The only thing I do is try to maintain the right atmosphere day by day during all of the shoot.

'It's something subtle, something inner: it's like a kind

of physical training. You have to fill yourself with the character's information and appropriate it, even subconsciously. And then certain attitudes surface naturally and that makes things work better on the set. Of course nobody has to know if I drank a beer or not during the five months of shooting *L.A. Confidential*, but the thing is, I have the impression that in the end, the effort shows.'

Russell was praised for his performance, with the *Washington Post* saying the actor had a 'unique and sexy toughness', and the *New York Observer* adding, 'Mr Crowe strikes the deepest registers with the tortured character of Bud White, a part that has had less cut out of it from the book than either Mr Spacey's or Mr Pearce's ... but Mr Crowe at moments reminded me of James Cagney's poignant performance in Charles Vidor's *Love Me or Leave Me* , and I can think of no higher praise.'

Roger Ebert, the famous 'two thumbs up' film critic, said, '*L.A. Confidential* is seductive and beautiful, cynical and twisted, and one of the best films of the year,' adding that 'Russell Crowe and Guy Pearce are two Australian actors who here move convincingly into star-making roles.'

Russell would remember of his time on the film, 'It's a really nice movie. Guy does a great job, Kevin Spacey is fabulous, Kim Basinger gives her best performance. I shouldn't say that because it sounds like I'm judging her work, but she takes you to a fluttering, emotional core that she hasn't brought you to for quite some time. She's been doing *Wayne's World* 2-type celebrity stuff and this is a real acting role. My favourite moments in the movie are hers.

'And it's got Danny DeVito in it – it's a wonderful ensemble cast. We went to Cannes together and the thing I really felt was how much we all liked each other, and we had a wonderful time of discussion and discovery on the movie. It's the first truly ensemble piece I've done in America. I don't mean that negatively but so often when you work here, you're in your corner, the other actor's in his corner and somebody rings a bell and you come out and do your business.'

CHAPTER TWELVE

CROWE MAKES HIS MARK

'Russell Crowe is one of the best actors I have ever worked with in my life.'

– Burt Reynolds

Just before work started on *L.A. Confidential*, Russell starred in the Australian road movie *Heaven's Burning* – a kinetic and Tarantino-like thriller. (It would be dubbed *Reservoir Dingos* by film critics.)

Russell got goosebumps while reading the script, but admitted that he was shocked at just how complex and convoluted it was. By the time he got to page 46, he remembered thinking, 'Damn, so much has happened and there's still another 50 pages to go.'

The film's producer, Al Clark, said, 'It's a road movie, yet it veers from being a traditional film of that genre. It's a thriller that doesn't feel an obligation to continually thrill, and it's a touching film about the way people can collide at a moment in their respective lives. The inherent poetry of the piece – which blends humour, excitement, romance and violence – stimulated all involved from the outset.'

Russell would play a petty getaway driver who ends up on a crazy adventure with a Japanese bride, played by Youki Kudoh.

The actress recalled she had an 'OK professional relationship' with the actor, adding, 'We spent very little time together on-set. He can be very difficult and certainly arrogant. When he's in a good mood, he's your next best friend, but on a bad day he's not easy to be around.'

It would be more than a year before Russell embarked on another film. 'I went through 71 scripts before I decided to do this one. It was over a year, from finishing a film called *Heaven's Burning*, before I found a script that had some sort of originality in it.'

He would add, 'Everyone wanted me to play a cop with De Niro, a cop with Michael Douglas, a cop with whoever. There's a rule of thumb that says, "It's really not how much is coming to the door, it's how much money is attached to it." But that's not why I'm in this. I thought, "I'm going to pull back a little bit. And just see what's out there." I just felt that there was progress to be made and if I just kept examining only what was being offered to me I would be able to make that progress. I ended up not working for 14 months!'

Eventually he ended up plumping for a role of a sheriff who refuses to carry a gun. 'I just thought it was very ironic for me to, after 14 months, play a lawman that holds conversation above the law. I'm a great fan of irony.'

Mystery, Alaska told the rousing tale of small Alaskan town getting behind their amateur ice hockey team after the New York Rangers agree to play a televised exhibition match against them.

'There's a great journey my character [John Biebe] has to go through in this film,' Russell said. 'For 13 seasons he's played in the Saturday game, then suddenly he's 34 years old, and a 17-year-old kid who's a better skater comes along and Biebe is taken off the team. As soon as he's removed from the game, the biggest hockey event Mystery has ever known happens when the New York Rangers come to play the town team. Internally he's falling apart, but he has to maintain the appearance of self-assurance.

'He doesn't wear a gun and doesn't carry handcuffs. He's not a violent person. He's elected the sheriff of the town, and it's something that he just does because he knows that, given this particular group of people, he can stay balanced. The only thing he gives up to the fact that he's an officer is he wears a badge sometimes. That's it.

'The other people who work for the sheriff's department – they're loaded, man. They have access to the weaponry, they use the weaponry, they wear the weaponry. He doesn't want to do that because in his mind his job is a totally different thing. I mean, he does have a rifle in the truck, because you never know when a polar bear's going to be doing some bad shit. But he's just not the sort of man who'd carry a pistol. A different kind of bloke.'

Directed by Jay Roach, with a script written by *Ally McBeal*'s David E Kelley, *Mystery, Alaska* saw Russell starring with Hollywood icon Burt Reynolds. To bond during the film, the pair went out on a drinking session. However, Reynolds revealed he had to cheat to keep up with his young actor. 'I could drink pretty good, but I used to cheat. Like when I filmed *Mystery, Alaska* with the Aussie. One night I said to the girl behind the bar, "Here's $100. Give me a vodka and tonic with a lime, but after that, alternate with water and lime." On the tenth round Russell grabbed the glass and took a swallow. Thank God it was the vodka. He said, "You're all right, mate."'

Roach would say about working with Russell, 'It's a kind of poetic approach to acting. That's what makes it so powerful. He's very controlled and disciplined about the externals – timing, blocking, choreography. But in addition to that he has a way of connecting to his subconscious that adds all these other layers of subtlety and nuance to what's on the outside. A four-second reaction shot from Russell can be equivalent to a full minute of dialogue. He can be supremely articulate without words.'

Mary McCormack, who plays Russell's wife in the movie, said, 'I just was so excited when I found out he was attached and I read the script. I just couldn't wait to go in and meet for it because I just think he's phenomenal.'

Disney decided during post-production to make the film less Russell-centric – something which Roach was unsure about. Surprisingly, Russell agreed.

'There was a debate, and Russell backed me up entirely. He felt like he had signed up for something that was an ensemble... He saw that the film would be better off if he was not elevated above the other characters. He became the kind of defender of the greater good.'

The film's small-town charm seemed to have an effect on the film critics. 'Consistently entertaining,' said the *San Francisco Chronicle*, while the *New York Times* said Russell's 'Rock of Gibraltar machismo anchors the film in decent common-sense values.'

Mystery, Alaska would also prove to be a financial boost. 'It wasn't until 1998, when I signed on to do *Mystery, Alaska*, that I went from the deepest red into the black,' Russell said. 'I'd stayed out of work for 14 months, because I wanted to do something important [slight giggle] after *L.A. Confidential*, and I got a 710 per cent pay rise between those two gigs, you know. And that's really important, that you [laughter], that you're patient enough to back your own talent at a certain point when it becomes real.'

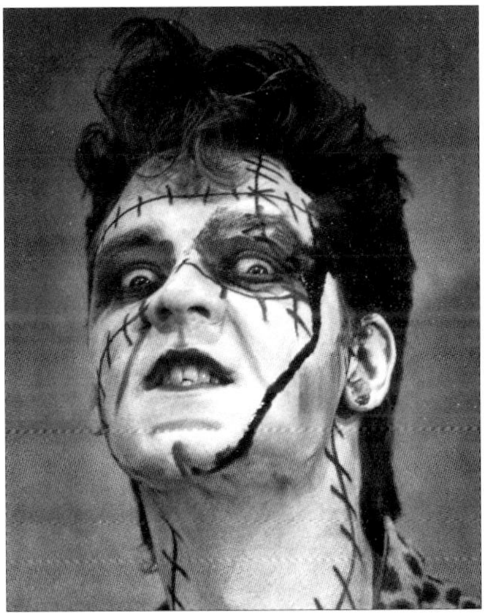

Above left: Russell Crowe as a young boy at Sydney Boys High School in Australia.

Above right: Russell posing for a shot in the 1980s.

Below left: Another headshot showing Russell as a teenager.

Below right: Russell looks terrifying in heavy make-up as 'Eddie' in the 1986 staging of *The Rocky Horror Show*.

Above left: Russell Crowe's grandmother, Joy Wemyss, proudly displays a picture of Russell as a school boy.

Above right: An old photograph of Russell's grandfather, Stan Wemyss, in Auckland New Zealand.

Below left: His first single cover, as Russ le Roq, called 'I Just Wanna Be Like Marlon Brando'.

Below right: Performing with his band Roman Antix in 1986.

Above: Like many famous Australian actors before and since, Russell appeared in the popular Aussie soap opera *Neighbours*. Here he is as Kenny Larkin, with Jason Donovan as Scott Robinson.

Below: Russell's first film role was alongside Danielle Spencer (who later became his wife) in *The Crossing* in 1990.

Above: Russell's starring role in *L.A. Confidential*, with Kim Basinger, finally brought him the mainstream fame and attention in the USA that many of his fans thought he deserved.

Below: He received a Best Actor Academy Award nomination for his part in *The Insider*, with Christopher Plummer.

Above: Roman General Maximus Decimus Meridius from the movie *Gladiator* was to become one of Russell Crowe's most enduring characters.

Below: Maximus' sword and scabbard from *Gladiator*.

Russell Crowe won the 2001 Academy Award for Best Actor in a Leading Role for *Gladiator*. Julia Roberts won the Oscar for Best Actress in the same year, for *Erin Brockovitch*.

Above left: Russell portrayed Nobel Laureate John Nash in *A Beautiful Mind* (2001). He was nominated once again for an Academy Award but lost out to Denzel Washington.

Above right: Greeting Prince Charles on the blue carpet at the premiere of *Master and Commander – The Far Side of the World* (2003).

Below: In character as heavyweight boxing champion James J Braddock in *Cinderella Man* (2005).

Russell married Danielle Spencer at their home in a lavish ceremony in Nana Glen, New South Wales Australia, on 7 April 2003. It was his 39th birthday.

CHAPTER THIRTEEN

RUSSELL COMES OF AGE

'I am an intense bastard when I'm doing my job.
I don't suffer fools and I don't mess around.
I want you to be ready, prepared, let's go mate.
Commit heart and soul.'

– Russell Crowe

If *L.A. Confidential* proved Russell was a movie star in the making, *The Insider* showed his acting chops as well. Russell remembers reading the script and loving every page of it. 'It was magnificent – one of the top three or four experiences of a read I've had – goosebumps and the whole bit.'

Russell loved the story – about a research scientist who comes under attack when he takes part in an exposé of the tobacco industry – and was particularly interested in the powers that the industry had. The film also served the notion that even with the truth out there, the sheer addictive power of cigarettes meant that stopping wasn't easy. To this day Russell still smokes but, he acknowledges,

'The fact that I could go through a project like that and haven't quit is an indication of the power of this addictive drug.

'After *The Insider* I know the exact chemical compounds in a commercial cigarette. But I've been smoking since I was ten. I know it's terrible but I'm a great fan of irony.'

So he loved the script, the idea of the film and its message. The only problem was he had no idea which part he was being asked to play.

The Insider was based on the true story of Dr Jeffrey Wigand, a tobacco company executive who revealed inside details on the US news show *60 Minutes* – details that would shake the tobacco industry to its core. However, his actions led to an intense smear campaign against him.

Looking at the script again, Russell just couldn't understand which part director Michael Mann wanted him for. The role of CBS producer Lowell Bergman was earmarked for Al Pacino, and Wigand was a bespectacled, chubby man in his fifties with thinning hair.

So Russell was shocked when he learned that he was being asked to play Wigand. 'I thought it was a silly mistake,' he remembered. 'There are many, many 50-year-old actors who are just marvellous, and I knew my co-star was going to be Al Pacino and you couldn't have a kind of paternal thing going on. They had to be peers, two men from different tribes trying really hard to get together and realising that it would be a lot easier if they really liked each other.

'Anyway, I'm part way through my speech to him about all this when Michael puts his hand on my chest and says, "I'm not talking to you because of your age. I'm talking to you because of what you have in here."'

To have that sort of belief in his talents touched Russell, and a meeting with the real-life Wigand sealed the deal – leaving him obsessed with making sure that Mann's faith was justified.

'I can remember being aware that there was something going on with *60 Minutes*. I read newspapers, but its significance wouldn't necessarily have affected me at that time, because it's a very intrinsically American story.

'I was lucky that Michael is a very organised man. I had access to the *60 Minutes* interview, to all of the different news reports that were run in different places. Still, I'd never played a real person before. I operate in a fictional world where, if you make a decision about your character, you can rationalise it any way you want. I realised that this was a real man who suffered a massive emotional impact because of this series of events. This guy's life changed completely, as did his opinion of himself and his self-esteem. So I had a meeting with Jeffrey. I asked a lot of really hard questions and it was a very emotional conversation, but he answered every question straight, looking me dead in the eye. I got up from that table and I thought to myself, "I must honour this man."'

Typically, Russell immersed himself in his character. He would listen to a six-hour tape of Wigand over and over again until he got it right. Two months before shooting, Mann would rarely leave Russell's side as they went through every detail about his character – his motives, his beliefs, his feelings – even down to what he wore and why. Eventually Russell told him, '"Michael, it's been a very interesting thing hanging out with you, but I need to learn the dialogue." I mean, he was driving me nuts.'

Talking about his character, he said, 'Playing somebody who's still alive and kicking is a tightrope job and it's complicated by the fact that Jeffrey is by no means a simple person.

'He's flawed, as we all are. He's a human being. Ultimately I think the social impact of his actions was a byproduct of a man trying to protect his family. Jeffrey didn't set out to be a hero, and he doesn't consider himself a hero now. There were true and real reasons in his mind for doing what he did, and most of them had to do with how one man protects himself and his family against a powerful corporation.'

If Mann's idea of casting Russell as Wigand surprised the actor, it stunned Pacino.

The veteran actor was initially unconvinced about Russell's casting, admitting, 'I thought at first he might be too young for the role. But then, as he started to play it in rehearsal, he was just transformed. I thought what he did was just brilliant.'

The pair would go on to become great friends. 'When you think of Al you tend to think of words like "intense",' Russell said, 'but he's a very relaxed fellow. He's very comfortable with himself and he's like a rumpled old blanket, you know?' – even more so after Russell got him a Louisville Slugger baseball bat personalised with Pacino's name.

'It cost about $40 and it was no big deal. So, I just left it in his trailer. I didn't know Al Pacino was the world's biggest baseball fan. I mean, it wasn't baseball season and we'd been watching basketball. He thought it was the greatest thing since sliced bread and he's like, "How did you know?"'

Pacino would return the favour, with Russell returning to his home in L.A. some time later to find boxes waiting near his door. 'They're from Al, and I start opening them up and it's a baseball pitching machine, the whole box and dice,' he says. 'A bloke that was working with me, a very dry fellow from Canada, said, "Well, Russell, thank God you didn't give him a pair of flippers!"'

Pacino wasn't the only actor impressed by Russell's talents. Christopher Plummer, said, '[I am] an enormous fan of Russell, who I think is probably the most versatile actor on the screen today. I mean, who would ever believe that he was Australian with that extraordinary performance in *L.A. Confidential* and also this one in which he is Mr Wigand to the nth degree. He is absolutely perfect; he transforms himself.'

But in Mann, Russell had found someone who was just as intense, dogged and driven on the film set. 'If any actor tells you that it's an easy gig working with him, they're lying through their teeth,' Russell said. 'Because he works really long hours and he's extremely intense. But he works on the principles that I've tried to hold on to in what I do: detail and collaboration... The bottom line is, he cares. And there's that kind of forthrightness about him.'

In another interview, he added, 'Working with Michael was a huge learning curve. I remember the first shot we did was of me walking through a doorway. Seventeen takes it took. And two days later we re-shot it. Eventually I was like, "Michael, don't spend the first ten takes looks at the fucking shadow on the wall. Don't even call me until you've worked out where the fucking shadow is. Don't waste this stuff, because I'm working from take one. I don't care who you've worked with before, mate. I don't need a warm-up, I'm ready."'

'I think I actually loosened him up a little, because later he said of me, and I'm not telling you this to blow my own trumpet, "All right, you've got the best Ferrari on the market. So what are you gonna do? Are you going to leave it in the garage or are you gonna get in and drive it?"'

The pair were so obsessed with every little detail that they even disputed at length how good a golfer Wigand was. Mann needed a scene to highlight Wigand's isolation, but at the same time to show elements of his self-discipline and drive. Hence, a scene at the driving range. But when Russell found out that the real Wigand wasn't as good a golfer as the one that Mann wanted, he believed it helped shape why Wigand never fitted in with the corporate future. He refused to budge on the issue.

Mann said of his experience working with Russell, 'He's totally an actor. Totally. I don't know what goes on between roles. Look at *On the Waterfront*, at *Streetcar* or even *The Young Lions*, and you see this raw, powerful talent that's dead serious and accomplished. That's Russell to me. I'm dying to work with him again.'

On its release, the film would come under fire from some critics over the order of events being changed for the film. This was a criticism that enraged Russell. 'What a load of bollocks. If we made movies in real time, we would be sitting in a cinema for four and a half years. I heard them saying, "Do you realise, in *The Insider* they compressed time?" What was all that about? OK, so Wigand was not on a golf driving range when he discovered people were following him. Stiff shit. Was he being followed? Yes. Were they doing it all the time? Yes. Did he feel pressure, which changed his life for ever? Yes. It incenses me in America that they can wave a red herring and people say, "Oh, I never believe in Hollywood movies." This is not Oliver Stone and his paranoid delusions of JFK. This is the truth. This is how corporate America operates, and it has to be cleaned up.'

It was a powerhouse performance by Russell – and one that saw him receive his best reviews at that time. 'Crowe has been made up to look like such an ashen-gray, middle-aged, Middle-American schlub that the occasional emergence of the actor's Australian accent doesn't matter. His performance is an unravelling knockout,' said the *San Francisco Examiner*, while the *Los Angeles Times* called him 'marvellous'.

They weren't alone in their admiration – Russell also received an Oscar nomination in 2000. 'I've watched the Academy Awards since I was a kid. I work in the business. I've worked in the business since I was six years old. It's a peer-voted system. It is the pinnacle of public achievement. And that doesn't mean that everybody who wins one is on the same level. But – I'm just talking about in terms of public perception of what you do – there's nothing bigger than that for my job.

'So, to have any kind of cool attitude towards it where you say (adopts fake American accent), "It's not important and I don't believe in competition between performers" and all that is odd. I mean, I don't believe in competition, but it's not that sort of competition. It's not a football match. It's a recognition thing. And it's not four or five people lined up to do a 100-metre sprint. It's four or five people who have already been acknowledged by their peers.'

Despite the ease with which Russell had put on weight for the part, he found it incredibly hard to lose again. 'I was aiming to gain 30lb, but a certain thing happens when you take on a sedentary lifestyle, and I ended up enjoying myself too much. I had a strict, medically controlled diet of bourbon and cheeseburgers. It took six weeks to take its toll. I thought, "Six weeks on, six weeks to get off," but once the film was over and I started to diet, it took five and a half months. I had my cholesterol checked at one point and I was in dangerous territory. I was surprised my body was taking it so seriously.'

And he would need to be in shape for his next role.

CHAPTER FOURTEEN

MAD MAXIMUS

'The great actors are never easy.'

– Ridley Scott

'There wasn't a single person in Los Angeles who thought, "Oh, great!" I mean, everybody was kind of looking at me as though I was retarded, patting me on the back and saying, "Well, you know, *L.A. Confidential* was great, wasn't it? At least you got to be in one good one..." And they were doing that all over town. I was like, "It's Ridley Scott! Are you aware of what he's capable of doing when it comes to creating a world?" Russell exclaimed to *Empire* magazine in a 2009 interview.

Gladiator was a film that should not have succeeded. Before it was released *Variety* said, 'Even if the film is a big hit, it's unlikely that the genre will come back in any significant way due to the high costs involved.'

How wrong they would be. Ridley Scott and Russell would resurrect the genre that had long been regarded as box-office poison – and it would be the blueprint for epics such as *Troy*, *The Lord of the Rings* and many others.

'There were a lot of epic films made in the 1940s and 1950s in Hollywood,' Scott said. 'After that people just stopped going to them and there was this fear of making period films for the big audience. That was one of the big challenges, actually. You couldn't make this film cheaply, but could you make it mainstream?'

He added, 'Everybody was quietly sniggering that Roman epics of this nature went out 45 years ago and that it wouldn't work. But I was absolutely confident about what I was going to do. Actually, I hadn't been that confident since *Alien*.

'It's funny, but when you are charging down to the fence and you know you are going to jump, there is a different level of exhilaration. And yes, we had shortfalls – we were constantly behind on the writing – but we were never behind on the production.'

Gladiator would go on to be one the most loved films of all time, and Russell Crowe's performance as the ousted Roman general Maximus would become iconic. However, like some of the world's most popular movies, it was a rocky path from the page to the screen.

'You know how they say an actor is the custodian of his role? Well, Russell is the bodyguard of his character. And he's on duty 24 hours a day!' So said *Gladiator* producer Douglas Wick. It was a part that would see

Russell with broken bones, tendon injuries and several cuts and bruises.

Make no mistake, this was his biggest role and in typical fashion it was a role that he would seize and wring every ounce of effort, passion and patience needed from himself and others while making the film.

'He would kill for his character,' Wick added. 'And Ridley would kill for the movie. So you have two very wilful people who are sometimes in disagreement.'

Russell recalled, 'On the set of *Gladiator*, I didn't have a very good relationship with the producers. I had a very good relationship with Ridley but the producers couldn't understand why I wouldn't just chill out. The reason I wouldn't chill out was because I knew that if I did fucking chill out, in those five minutes something stupid would now be in the movie. Like, they were trying to get me to do a love scene, and I'm saying to them, "What we're doing here is about the vengeance of a man whose wife has been killed – you cannot have him stop off for a little bit of nookie on the way."'

Ridley said of his reason for casting him, 'Russell was really always my first choice. I noticed [him] maybe five years ago in *Romper Stomper* and I thought he was somebody worth watching. Once in a while somebody comes along, and he's got all those little elements that accumulate together into making him.'

He added during the film's premiere in Los Angeles, 'I

just thought Russell was fresh, a new generation – he's a man definitely on his way up.'

Screenwriter David Franzoni would say, 'A bunch of us were sitting in Steven's [Spielberg's] offices just jamming like jazz musicians, throwing names around. There were really only two crucial questions – who was going to direct and who was going to play the gladiator Maximus.

'Well, we thought Mel Gibson, but we knew he wasn't going to do it, and Russell was in our minds because we had all seen *L.A. Confidential*. And as soon as he signed on, there really wasn't any further question about it. He was the guy.'

It was a part that Russell was very close to refusing. At that point he was working on the role of *The Insider*. 'I was ignoring it because I was working. The two things weren't coming together in my head. I thought it would be a load of crap – poncing around in a tunic,' he is reported to have said.

During his make-up sessions for *The Insider*, he and Mann would chat about the film, the shooting for that day and so forth. Talk would inevitably extend to other things like future projects and so forth. And when Mann heard that Russell was thinking about turning down the part, the director said he would be crazy not to work with Scott. 'You should take this Ridley Scott project more seriously,' Mann told him. 'It is my belief that Ridley Scott is in the top two per cent of shooters who existed in the power of the cinema.'

Scott was a hugely influential director thanks to films like *Alien* and *Blade Runner*. But his recent CV, which included the likes of *G.I. Jane* and *White Squall*, had led some to suggest that his powers to thrill audiences had waned. But after meeting with him, Russell was not only convinced by the director but put his faith in a film that really hadn't got a working script at that moment.

'Usually, I make my decision based on the script,' he explained. 'I make films that give me goose bumps when I read them. But that one I chose because of the concept. They called me and said, "We're not going to show you the script, because we don't think you'll like it as it is. But here's the idea: Ridley Scott, 185 AD, and at the beginning of the film, you are a Roman general." That was enough to convince me to talk to Ridley because it spoke to my imagination and it was a chance to work with a guy Michael Mann calls one of the best film-makers in the history of cinema. And there they had me...'

The film came about through screenwriter Franzoni. He had been given a three-picture deal with DreamWorks studio based on the success of his screenplay *Amistad* with them. He mentioned the idea to Steven Spielberg, who asked three questions, Franzoni recalled. '"My *Gladiator* movie – it was about ancient Roman gladiators, not American, Japanese, whatever else?" "Yes," I said. "Taking place in the ancient Coliseum?" "Yes." "Fighting with swords and animals to the death and such?" "Yes." "Great! Let's make this movie."'

Franzoni had had the idea for the film after reading the 1958 novel *Those About to Die* by Daniel Mannix. His screenplay had the protagonist Narcissus (as he was named then) become something of a superstar gladiator who is sponsored by the Golden Pompeii Olive Oil Company. An advertising slogan has the line: 'Narcissus would kill for a taste of Golden Pompeii Olive Oil.'

'My vision from the beginning was – this is not *Ben Hur*. It's *All Quiet on the Western Front*,' Franzoni said. 'This is a grown-up movie about war, death and life in Rome – the life of a gladiator.'

However, he also went on to say, 'I would have liked to have had more fun with this' – a reference to the elimination of the Olive Oil Company endorsement.

John Logan wrote the second draft of the script, turning it into a more serious affair and changing Narcissus' name to Maximus, before William Nicholson became the third writer on the film.

Why the changes? *Gladiator Film and History* author Martin Winkler notes that 'it seems rather likely that it was Scott who turned the film from Franzoni's socio-political, delightfully bizarre action film into a more sombre study of war, death and life in Rome.'

The screenplay would go through many more changes, even when the cameras were rolling. 'Last-minute tweaking of the script and a new ending helped the production to stay on track,' explained producer Douglas Wick.

Gladiator would be the start of a blossoming relationship between Russell and Scott. Almost immediately, Scott realised the full extent of working with an actor like Russell. Straight away, Russell expected to collaborate. 'There were still details to hammer out. We sort of had to take the script apart to rebuild it into a narrative that we could agree upon, Ridley and I.'

Of course, it could be argued that a script with just a heavy concept and an outline is perfect for Russell, who is vocal about shortcomings in a script. He and Scott came up with several ideas to benefit the film. Russell remembered one of his school's Latin mottos – *Veritate et Virtute* – and walked up to Scott with an idea.

'I went to Ridley, 'cause I was looking for something instead of just saying, "Goodbye". Something that felt gladiatorial... military... something that felt part of the time. And so I remembered that school motto and I converted it, and I said it to him in Latin. And he sort of raised an eyebrow, and he took his cigar out of his mouth and goes, "What's that mean, then?" I said, "Strength and Honour," and he goes, "Say that!"'

He added, 'Possibly, a lot of the stuff that I have to deal with now in terms of my quote unquote "volatility" has to do with that experience. Here was a situation where we got to Morocco with a crew of 200 and a cast of 100 or whatever, and I didn't have anything to learn. I actually didn't know what the scenes were gonna be. We had, I think, one American writer working on it, one

English writer working on it, and of course a group of producers who were also adding their ideas and then Ridley himself. And then, on the occasion where Ridley would say, "Look, this is the structure for it – what are you gonna say in that?" then I'd be doing my own stuff as well. And this is how things like, "Strength and honour" came up. This is how things like, "At my signal, unleash hell," came up. Um, the name Maximus Decimus Meridius – it just flowed well, you know?'

One battle Russell would lose, however, was his belief that Maximus should have a Spanish accent. 'I wanted to do Antonio Banderas with better elocution. But they wouldn't let me. They didn't want people to be distracted by it. But I felt when you say you're Spanish 50 times in the course of the movie, I should be doing the accent. Instead, basically everybody in the movie does, you know, Royal Shakespeare Company two pints after lunch.'

'Russell was not well behaved. He tried to rewrite the entire script on the spot,' said an insider on the film. 'Russell could act like a jerk but he's an artist. He'd have his little meltdown and stomp off for half an hour.'

Whatever his actions on set, it's clear that he came bounding into the film with a different outlook from action stars of the past – the Stallones, the Schwarzeneggers and the Willises.

'Those kinds of action heroes leave me cold and it really gives me a pain in the arse,' he said in an interview.

'As far as they're concerned, the big mistake is their monolithism. A good soldier is a man who can control his fear a little bit longer than the others. Those heroes are never scared of anything.

'The approach to my character is different, more subtle. Maximus is a general. To help me playing the character, I gave him a past. The past of a nine-year-old kid who would have joined the Roman army, would have climbed one grade after another, would have been noticed during battles and would have become – and the film starts here – a general who is faithful to Marcus Aurelius. He's a man who truly built his life, who has a wife and a son, vineyard and olive groves, who doesn't give a damn about the fact that his amour is shining or not. He knows what is important and what is not, and his life is even more precious because of that. It can't be more different to the action heroes you're talking about. They're crude characters with a gun in their hands!'

About Maximus he adds, 'I think he's a man guided by love – the love he feels for his Emperor Marcus Aurelius, for the Roman Empire, for his wife and his son. Each time he comes to a decision, it's consistent. He's a straight man, but he's also a warrior, a fiery and rough man who is able to split in two his enemy with a blow of his sword, because at that time soldiers bodily fought and that's the way Maximus leads his life.'

It was a physically and mentally draining film shoot that would see Russell exhausted by the demands of both the character and studio politics. He would storm off set but then he would make sure everyone, from runners upwards, got their rugby fleeces of his team. Generous to a fault one minute, moody the next.

He would have impromptu rugby games with the cast and crew, watch football games with them, and even take bets on Manchester United winning the 1999 Champions League cup final despite being 1-0 down with minutes to go. When Manchester United did go on to win, he ran around spraying beer over everyone.

Charlie Allan, the chief executive of the Clanranald Trust, played a German warrior in *Gladiator*, and the pair have been friends ever since. 'I first met Russell on the set of *Gladiator* when he came over to talk to me and asked if I owned a motorcycle or just owned the leather jacket. I replied, "Two Harleys, mate." Russell then told me about his own Harley and the special paint job he has on it with permission from Harley Davidson themselves. We hit it off from there and he invited me to meet him for a beer after the shoot.

'I thought he was softly spoken and a really nice likeable guy. A man's man, into his bikes and music, and down to earth. I had seen him in previous works and you would think that I would have had an opinion about him but I realised I didn't. I immediately thought, "I like this guy, this guy is OK."'

On the set of *Gladiator*, the conditions were very difficult but Russell's energy helped. Allan recalled, 'The weather was much more cold, the light never really came as it was February and the mud was up to our knees having been churned up with deforesting and preparing the set.

'It was a perfect setting for a battle in the early morning. The suspense could be felt as we all knew the clash and hand-to-hand fighting was about to begin. The atmosphere was electric and everyone had a buzz about them. There were approximately 1,500 people on this small set, not including crew. The sound carried as it travelled slowly in the cold air and the smoke machines did their work well.

'Morale dipped a little but a game of rugby with a makeshift ball helped put the spark back in there. The Celts lost the battle but won the rugby.'

The producers didn't know what to do with Russell. Frustration at their actor's unwillingness to toe the party line – there were even reports of him getting into brawls with the locals – was matched only by their lack of understanding of exactly why he was doing this. He was not demanding money or actor perks – he was just becoming a nuisance.

Russell said, 'I've been told that Jeffrey Katzenberg rang Michael Mann and said, "Look, this guy is just not rolling with the punches as we want him to, so what's it all about?" And Michael said, "Well, if you're having problems like that with Russell, then you've got to know that you should just follow him." Jeff said, "Is this about fucking ego and stuff?" and Michael started laughing. Because vanity doesn't come into it. Is it right for the fucking character?'

And it's clear that he threw himself into the character. To get into the role of being a leader among men, Russell organized a 6,500km (4,000-mile) motorbike ride around Australia with his pals.

Then there were the injuries. 'I cracked a bone in my foot. I got a little fracture in my hip. Both my bicep tendons popped out – luckily, at different times, so I still had one arm I could use. It's the nature of doing these kinds of things... I love these things, which are quite dangerous to do. They may look simple, but galloping down a hill, for example – horses won't do it by themselves unless you tell them to do it.

'I actually had one hell of an experience. You felt we were using more napalm than *Apocalypse Now*. One of the flame pots had fallen over and nobody noticed, so when they said "Action!" and pushed the button to start the fires, my horse got a jet of fire right up his behind, and he didn't like it very much and started going backwards down the hill.

'He had blinkers on, I had a helmet on, we couldn't see behind us. He backed into a tree and then another tree and a branch pierced my cheek, going all the way through.'

In an interview with *Film Review*, he added, 'Filming was a physically trying experience. At the outset, on paper, we had planned a break of around seven days between the combat scenes in order to have time to recuperate and be ready to do it again. But after all was said and done, with all the changes in plans that happen during filming, we found ourselves doing them one after another. I fought tigers during the day, and prepared for the next scene in the evenings with the fight trainer, the master at arms, horse trainer... physically, it left scars. But looking back, it was also what made it an unforgettable experience. But at the time, when you look at yourself in the mirror and you have your biceps tendon coming out from your shoulder on the wrong side, you ask yourself, "What am I doing here ?"'

The thrilling fight sequence with tigers (originally to be rhinos) prowling about also proved to be a hairy experience. 'They are magnificent creatures, but they don't always do what you ask them to,' Russell remembered. 'Meanwhile, it's been 12 days to film scenes with them when we planned for six. There were some trying moments. They used a chain held by three men to limit their forward movements. That works very well as long as the tiger wants to go forward. One day when the guys were pulling a little hard, the tiger said, "If you don't want me to go there, I can just as well come towards you."

'Two of them did what they had been told to do in that case: stay still and cover your head. But the third one panicked. He got two steps and the tiger was on him. Bang, on the ground! And the tiger was just playing. But you know how cats are... he is playing one moment and the next he can tear your head off.

'Another time, at the moment when the tigers' door opens, I was in the middle of fighting Sven [Ole Thorsen]. He was wearing his helmet, a really heavy thing, without peripheral vision. It appeared to me that the signal for the tigers was given a little too soon and I started to accelerate the rhythm. Our movements are planned like choreography. Because he couldn't see what was happening, when the tempo increased, Sven stopped to ask what happened. And before he knew it, the tiger was on him. It gave him a big swat on the backside. Luckily for him, it was one of the tigers whose claws had been removed. Otherwise, he would have had those scars for the rest of his life. After that, I can tell you that he really learned to work better with the helmet on!'

Despite the injuries, it's clear that Russell found something of the perfect working relationship with Scott. 'Seeing him orchestrate five different camera crews on five monitors, you know, with 3,000 extras – he'd say, "I want this here, I want that there. OK, now if you can bring me in the 500 German guys – and get hairy guys in the front. Not those little skinny ones, hairy guys!" He gives everybody instructions and he gets ready for another take and I say, "What should I do?" And he says, "Oh, no. You're fine."

'Ridley's reputation as a director is that no matter how difficult the story he's telling, he will finish on time and on budget. He's also a very straight talker, and so am I. If you're going to take a leap of faith like this movie, then these are the people to do it with.'

He would add, 'When Ridley realised just how much he could get from me, he was like "Whoa". He realised that he could have as much fun with me as he wanted, because there's no level of anything that I can't go to. There's nothing I can't do.'

Joaquin Phoenix, who played Roman Emperor Commodus, said of his experiences working on the film, 'Initially, I was not sure where to start. Going through the first rehearsal dressed in my jeans, I was thinking, "What the hell am I doing?" Then I put on the layers of armour and I felt different. Costume and make-up really do make a big difference, especially because I'm obsessed with the physicality of the character.

'At the beginning I permed up my hair twice, to look like the young, scraggy prince in waiting. Then, as he became emperor, I cut my hair and stopped going to the gym. I wanted to put on a few pounds, because I wanted some of that lazy decadence that would come from being an emperor.'

Because of the stars involved in the film (the cream of British thespian talent, including Derek Jacobi, Oliver Reed and Richard Harris), Phoenix was struck by nerves.

Phoenix remembered saying, '"Russ, I'm so nervous." He just took me aside and he gave me words of support.'

Russell said of Phoenix, 'Joaquin is a lovely guy, but

nervous. He lacks a little self-confidence. Ridley would say, "You're now the emperor and you have to walk out in the middle of the Colosseum." And Joaquin would say, "But I'm a lad from Florida. What do you want me to do? Wave?"'

Luckily, Richard Harris came up with a plan.

'Harris,' Russell recalled, 'with all his years and knowledge of the cinema and his wisdom, said quite simply, "Let's get him drunk!" And the drinking session seemed to do the trick. Joaquin kind of realised, "Oh yeah, I'm an actor, so I can relax a little bit."'

During filming of *Gladiator*, Russell struck up a friendship with Harris, a legendary hellraiser. Talk about two peas in a pod! After a heavy night out, the great actor turned to Russell and said, 'You're a good night in one man, Crowe. I think I'm going to like you.'

In 2001, Harris said, 'What goes on now is so stupid. It's like creating importance around themselves. On the other hand, I like a guy that a lot of people don't like here in the States. And that's Russell Crowe. A down-to-earth guy. When I was finishing up on *Gladiator*, Russell and I kind of hung around together. He'd come to my pubs, he'd walk in, sit down, no fuss. He took me to his pubs, the Australian pubs in London, no fuss. That's what I like. And I hope he stays like that. And that's why people don't like Russell in Hollywood. He says what he feels, and he doesn't play the game. He's really from my generation, from the O'Toole, Harris and Burton generation. You know, no bull.'

In 2006, Russell travelled from Australia to a small Irish village to watch the unveiling of a bronze statue of Richard Harris, who sadly passed away in 2002. He said, 'I met Richard at a time in his life when he was probably reflective of what he had done over the time he had spent on the planet. He very kindly passed a lot of wisdom on to me.' Russell even sang a song at the ceremony.

He says now, 'I miss him especially when I go to England. Because I'd invariably ring him up at The Savoy [Hotel, where Harris kept a suite] or maybe go to the bar there and just call his room. I was extraordinarily lucky with Richard. I would be able to find him in London because I knew his haunts. Even though it's a big city there were specific places that he liked to go. I'm not sure if it was really driven by me or by him.

'On the first night I met him, he said: "Crowe, is it true you were born in New Zealand but choose to live in Australia? Right, right. So I can talk to you in hushed and reverent tones about the All Blacks, and I can yell abuse at you about the bloody Wallabies!"

Talking about Reed, who passed away during filming of *Gladiator*, he said, 'Oliver was very disciplined while we were in Morocco, which was great. It's a very hard place to shoot, and I think this movie is a wonderful memorial to his contributions to cinema. I think it's his best performance in years.'

Despite his critical success with *L.A. Confidential* and *The Insider*, *Gladiator* was Russell's big break as a genuine movie star. 'People were still patting me on the back and patronising me: "It's OK. You might get another job,"' he remembered. But after seeing a final cut of the movie, he had every hope the film would be a big success.

CHAPTER FIFTEEN

IN THE PUBLIC EYE

'Steve McQueen, Charles Bronson – people like that. We haven't seen stars like that here for some tim. He's maybe it.'

– screenwriter David Franzoni

At the 2000 Oscar ceremony Russell received the Academy Award for Best Actor for his performance in *Gladiator*. Wearing his grandfather's medals, he said, 'My grandfather's name was Stan Wemyss. He was a cinematographer in the Second World War. My uncle David, David William Crowe, he died last year at the age of 66. I'd like to thank the Academy for something which is pretty surprising and dedicate it to two men who still continue to inspire me. I'd also like to thank my mum and dad, who I just don't thank enough I suppose.

'But really folks, I owe this to one bloke and his name is Ridley Scott. You know, when you grow up in the suburbs of Sydney or Auckland, or Newcastle like Ridley or Jamie Bell… or the suburbs of anywhere, you know a dream like this seems kind of vaguely ludicrous and completely unobtainable. But this moment is directly connected to those childhood imaginings. And for anybody who's on the downside of advantage and relying purely on courage… it's possible.'

Talking about his Oscar win, Russell said, 'To be honest, when you're younger and cooler, you say those sort of things don't mean anything, but then on the day when they pat you on the back and they say, "Look, mate, we're noticing what you're doing – thanks very much," you think of the people who spent a life in the cinema and didn't receive that kind of accolade, and it's sort of a humbling experience. And it's very nice and all that. But it doesn't change the way I do things.'

Everyone who played their part in Russell blossoming into the fierce and passionate actor he had become was delighted with his success. His old musician pal Tom Sharplin can remember phoning the actor to congratulate him, but it was Russell's mother who answered. She told him, 'You should have been here, Tom. He'd never have got this far if it wasn't for you.'

His grandmother Joy said, 'I've never been a believer in ghosts, but when I saw the medal on Russell's chest I knew Stan was with me here. I felt his presence so strongly in the room with me. Stan would have sat here crying, as I was, with pride. He thought the world of Russell and he was really soft hearted.'

Joy also revealed that she got too scared watching *Gladiator*. 'It was a wonderful movie but I couldn't take it when I thought he was going to be killed. I stood up and shouted, "No, no, leave him alone! Don't hurt him!" People were laughing and I heard Russell say, "Joy, sit down."

It's proof of how enduring the film is that despite Russell's character dying at the end, there is still talk of a sequel featuring Maximus. In 2006, Scott said, 'I will probably do a sequel to *Gladiator*. The only problem is Russell Crowe was such a powerful presence and, of course, Maximus dies at the end. We'll have to get Russell back somehow.'

Not that Russell and Scott ever regretted killing Maximus off. They knew that was the only way the film could have ended – although it was an outcome that the studio would have preferred to avoid.

'Although *Gladiator* is a movie about vengeance, it's also a movie about death and that's why Max had to die,' Russell explained. 'When we killed him, the studio just about had ten puppies. They couldn't believe it, and we had to keep that piece of information aside for a while. But when they saw it in place, they realised that in the fullness of what Ridley had created, it was the only fair way to end that film.

'I mean, if you ended that film and Max jumps up and says, "It's only a flesh wound! Just give us a couple of aspirins", then the journey won't be as fulfilling.'

Russell had made it, but his hunger for the job was even

fiercer than when he was starting out and yearning for success. In an interview with *Sony Magazine*, he said, 'Once, when I was earning about 26 cents a movie, someone asked, "What would you do if you were earning $10 million a movie?" And I went, "Retire. Go home, pay the bills, look after Mum and Dad and say goodbye to work."

'But of course the reality of the thing is that you are not in this business for the bucks anyway. And I know that will come across as being incredibly pretentious and something that people will assassinate me for, but this gig's a calling, man, especially for people that do it in a public way for more than four or five years.

'You know, you put up with all the crap that comes with this job and you have to love it at its core. And I dig it, man; I think it's a privilege making films. It's the most expensive, creative medium on the planet and it is a privilege for me to do it. I give it my best and I don't have any problems whatsoever in standing up in front of a group of people and saying, "I take making movies seriously and if you don't then golly, you obviously won't like my movies." That's about it, really.'

Gladiator thrust Russell into the spotlight. He would find this constant attention on him incredibly intrusive – never more than during filming of his next movie, *Proof of Life*. He told the *Vancouver Sun*, 'I've just decided to do a movie with Taylor Hackford... where I play an Australian. It's taken a long time, but now I get to play a serious, tertiary-educated, sentient character who speaks with my native accent in a big-budget Hollywood film.'

'It's a pretty similar situation to the other scripts that I read and end up doing in that there's something within the stories – new or fresh. There is a lot of information in this story that we haven not seen before.'

Playing an Australian pleased Russell hugely. He had been irked by the press back home suggesting that he had turned his back on his country because of his success in Hollywood and his seeming desire to use American accents.

His ire was further stoked during an award ceremony when Bryan Brown listed the names of 'Australian actors who have not only contributed to Australian cinema but also to the Australian identity' and pointedly left out Nicole Kidman – who was present at the ceremony – and his *Blood Oath* co-star.

When Russell presented an award soon after the perceived slight, he said, 'Bryan, on behalf of Nicole Kidman and myself, we forgive you. You're ignoring the fact that, based on hard work, sweat and commitment, there is a bridge that exists between the Australian and the film industry.'

Proof of Life, which was based on the *Vanity Fair* article *Adventures in the Ransom Trade*, tells the story of hostage negotiator Terry Thorne in his quest to rescue an American engineer. Complications arise when he begins to develop an attraction to the hostage's wife Alice.

Talking about the differences between his character

Terry Thorne and that of Maximus in *Gladiator*, he said, 'Just the physicality of Terry Thorne in *Proof of Life,* for example. It's much more contemporary than the body of Maximus. He's gone to a gym. He's worked on farms and he's big and round and everything. Terry's got this striation because he works out at the gym and he's got X amount of time in the day to do that kind of physical work. The more you inform yourself and fuel the internal engine that drives the character, then you get to the point where you can be standing on a hillside, saying no dialogue, but completely communicating to every person that's watching that film all of those peaks of desperation, joy, sadness and acceptance without saying a single word.'

Talking about Terry, Russell told the *Vancouver Sun*, 'He's got a very good bedside manner. He's very calm and reassuring to the client, but there is a distance. He has his business sincerity level but at the same time what happens in our story cuts through his ordinarily objective persona where he is affected more emotionally by the people involved.'

Explaining why he cast Russell in the film, Hackford said, 'Russell had done *L.A. Confidential*, which I was impressed with. However, I'd heard that Russell had two films in the can, *The Insider* and *Gladiator* that no one had seen.

'I called both directors, who are my colleagues, and asked them a major favour: to go into their editing rooms and see Russell's unreleased work. I first saw Ridley Scott's *Gladiator*. I fully expected Ridley to paint a huge canvas, but I was particularly impressed by how Russell Crowe dominated that canvas. His physicality was palpable, but there was also a real intelligence shining through all that physicality.

'Then I went across town into Michael Mann's editing room and saw an actor who'd gained 45lb playing an entirely non-physical, intellectual character involved in a crisis of conscience. I thought, "This guy is an incredible actor and he's definitely going to be a star!"'

It would be a gruelling shoot – with Hackford desperate to have as many location-based shots as possible. They would film parts of the movie in Poland ('It's cold enough to freeze the nuts off a brown dog on a rusty chain at 50 yards before he had time to eat his tucker,' said Russell) and Ecuador.

'When Russell Crowe crawls through a dense cloud forest, there's rain and mud all over him. This is real. It's not called a rain forest for nothing,' Hackford said.

The cast and crew would have to put up with arduous conditions, altitude sickness, fear of landslides and low visibility. 'Eventually, all of us started to feel like hostages' – and Russell and Hackford would regularly clash on set.

As William Prochnau would write in *Proof of Life: A Writer's Notebook*: 'Of all the super-egos who careened testily and creatively off each other on the set of *Proof of Life*, none were more complex than the director, Taylor Hackford. No one could rise so suddenly to brutalising verbal assaults or retreat so abruptly to emotional, almost self-flagellating but genuine apologies.

'Some who work for him tell you freely that they hate him and just as certainly that they will return to his side for his next movie.'

The pair's relationship would wobble 'between raw-edged and comical', with Russell forced to wait in a trailer for half a day as Hackford ran over the shooting schedule that day on a minor scene with an extra.

Russell would re-pay him by turning up late for filming on a handful of occasions. One instance saw him arrive late on a Sunday morning after a heavy night's partying, saying, 'Sorry mate, sermon ran long.'

The love scenes were cut. 'Hackford admits he filmed a more explicit love scene but that it has been exorcised from the final print', Russell explained.

'This was completely my decision,' the director said. 'There was no pressure from Meg, or Russell for that matter – and certainly not from the studio. I screened the film with and without the love scene and had to go with the version that worked best for audiences... Too much romance detracts from the action-adventure.

'If I wanted to be sensational I could have inserted the scene, but it would have detracted greatly. I wanted the relationship between the characters to be tenuous and ambiguous.'

As ever, Russell would do as many stunts as possible, telling US chat-show host Jay Leno, 'Yeah, well if I can give the director as many 100 per cent shots as I can, then the audience stays right within the story. They don't say, "Oh, hold on a second, that body shape is a little bit different," or "His nose is bigger" or whatever. So I think it just adds to the excitement of the movie.'

Russell received training for his part from former SAS members, and claimed to camp out in the Ecuadorian rainforests rather than stay in a plush hotel. 'I made a barbecue out of an oil can and stole food off the caterer. I'd wave as everybody drove off in the evening and wave as they drove back in the morning and people were like, "Are you crazy? There's wild cats in the jungle." Quite frankly I will take the wild cats over the Ecuadorian drivers any day.'

It's probably safe to assume that his bodyguard (former SAS man Adam Hamon) was with him at the time.

The SAS consultant was Thell Reed – the same man who had taught Russell how to quick-draw and shoot for *The Quick and the Dead*. Because Russell had had little to no experience with firearms before that Western, Reed reasoned, 'No bad habits to unlearn. Now he shoots better than most SAS men.'

As proof of that, Russell was adamant about carrying a firearm in certain parts of Ecuador. 'The Ecuadorian paratrooper colonel assigned to the movie tried to talk him out of it. No need. Dangerous. Crowe would have none of that – he, Reed and Crowe's bodyguard wanted gun permits. The colonel warned him that they had to pass a rigid test at the firing range. The top score was five. The colonel got a four. The three outsiders got fives,' said Prochnau.

Russell's insistence on doing his own stunts came back to haunt him in one scene.

Said Prochnau, 'Crowe was decked out each day in jungle khakis, his face painted in green-and-black camouflage streaks. He did his own stunts, which meant a lot of sloshing in the mud and combat rolls down hillsides with an M-4 rifle.

'In one, he did a 30ft roll, coming up weapon ready at the hut in which David Morse was being held captive. In his first practice, the roll went perfectly, then ended behind the hut in a terrible clatter and a roar of "Mutha-fucka!" that echoed through the jungle hills. Crowe had rolled over three unseen logs. Everyone rushed toward him. Was he hurt? An old injury, he said, shaking it off. But it wasn't that old – a shoulder injured making *Gladiator* and, unknown to anyone, the same injury that later would require surgery and force him out of his next movie. He went back and did the same scene six more times.'

Tragedy struck the set early on in the shooting. Morse's stand-in Will Gaffney – a 29-year-old teacher who had been on holiday – and five extras were filming a 'minor' scene when their truck careened off the road and down a 350ft ravine. While the extras survived, Gaffney sadly died. Hackford would later say, 'I don't think any film is worth losing your life for. It's something I'll always carry with me.'

As perfectly fine as it is, the hostage drama would just be a signpost in Russell's career – overshadowed by two events in Russell's life.

The first, bizarrely, involved a real-life hostage situation that was far more exciting than the film. Because of *Gladiator*'s success and the subsequent Oscar win, Russell became something of an American hero, which was why he became a target for extremists.

'That was the first conversation in my life that I'd ever heard the phrase Al Qaeda,' Russell said. 'It was something to do with some recording picked up by a French policewoman, I think, in either Libya or Algiers. I don't think I was the only person. But it was about – and here's another little touch of irony – taking iconographic Americans out of the picture as a sort of cultural-destabilization plan.

'[The FBI] picked up on something they thought was really important, and they were following it through. They were fucking serious, mate. What are you supposed to do? You get this late-night call from the FBI when you arrive in Los Angeles, and they're like absolutely full-on. "We've got to talk to you now, before you do anything. We have to have a discussion with you, Mr Crowe."

'We just arrived in Los Angeles, and we got contacted by the FBI, and they arrived at the hotel we were staying at. They went through this big elaborate speech, telling us that for the whole time we were going to be in America, they were going to be around and part of life.

'You know – oh, I shouldn't say things like this – I do wonder if it was some kind of PR thing to attract sympathy toward me, because it seemed very odd. Suddenly, it looks like I think I'm fucking Elvis Presley, because everywhere I go there are all these FBI guys around.'

Despite his genuine fears, he can laugh about it now. 'Oh yeah, there was a point where they said they thought the threat had probably or possibly been overstated, and then they started to question their sources, and blah, blah, blah. But I don't know how it was resolved, you know? But they were serious about it. And what can you say? I mean, gee, there were a lot of man-hours spent doing that gig, so the least I can say is, "Thank you very much."

'I think it was a bit odd. But I also thought, "Mate, if you want to kidnap me, you'd better bring a mouth gag. I'll be talking you out of the essential philosophies you believe in the first 24 hours, son. I might chew through the first one, too, so be prepared."'

The second thing that would overshadow the movie was his real-life romance with Meg Ryan, who had played the hostage's wife. The actress's marriage to Dennis Quaid was seen as one of the most solid in Hollywood, so news of the Crowe and Ryan romance sent shockwaves around showbiz circles.

Quaid filed for divorce soon after pictures surfaced of Russell and Ryan showing obvious affection – stroking each other's hair and hands – at a David Bowie concert.

Ryan's mother, Susan Jordan, said, 'Everyone else was

so surprised when Meg's affair became public, but I suppose I wasn't. It was clear her marriage was going nowhere.

'She's running all over London with Russell and she's having a picture taken with him and David Bowie. To me this is not a woman who is ashamed of what she is doing.

'Meg always liked macho men. I think Russell is exciting and giving her something that was clearly lacking in her marriage.'

It would later transpire that the marriage had not been as solid as it looked. But the damage had already been done – with Russell painted as a home-wrecker.

The public vitriol towards Ryan came as something of a surprise for someone who, at that time, was very much an American sweetheart. Talking about the backlash, she said, 'It's a very big surprise in life when you learn that not everyone is rooting for you. It's a very scary thing when you figure that out. I never imagined that worrying about what other people think of me would be a big part of my day. But, when you get that much negativity thrown at you, you go, "Whew, I've got to cope with that." Nothing I heard in the press resembled the truth. What an insight for me.'

Russell added in 2002, 'The situation with Meg was simpler and at the same time more complicated. But all the accusations that were levelled towards her and this residual reputation that I now have, all of that was undeserving. It was a much more simple and human situation, and sooner or later people won't need to talk about it any more.'

Their split – Ryan ending the relationship over a phone

call – came at a time when there was fevered speculation over whether theirs would be one of the biggest showbiz weddings of the year. Reports had arisen because the huge bash planned for Russell's farm – an event that had many revellers, marquee tents and caterers lined up for the excitement. What was overlooked was that the bash was an annual Christmas event held by Russell for his family and friends. It seems the press were hoping that if they wished for an A-list wedding hard enough, one would come.

Russell was badly shaken by the parting. A friend told the media, 'He virtually didn't leave his room for two days. His mother was really worried, but by the time his friends started arriving for the party he had composed himself. He joined in the drinking, swimming and barbecues, but Meg's name was never mentioned.'

The split was in part attributed to him refusing to spend less time in Australia. He said afterwards, 'I owe her an apology for not being as flexible as I might have been. I don't think that I'll ever make that mistake again.'

In another interview he added, 'The bottom line is, I have a big life here. I've got to be here. When I'm off the hook with the schedules, I have to come home. Meg has the same needs. We both have huge schedules. She is a searcher. She's got an incredibly inquisitive mind, so it was very easy for us to be in the same room together for hours and hours, just talking. That was very special.'

The home-wrecker tag attributed to Russell hit him hard, and it was only six years later, when Ryan talked to

Oprah Winfrey, that she admitted he didn't deserve that. 'It was a very unhealthy marriage and it was pretty much not a happening marriage for a very long time. I probably should have left much earlier.

'I'm very sad that it all had to come apart in the way that it seemed to have. It was never about another man, it was only about what my and Dennis's relationship just couldn't sustain. He [Crowe] wasn't a home-wrecker and he took a lot of heat for that and he had a lot of grace, frankly, about not talking about things that he knew were going on in my marriage and I'll be very grateful for him for a long time for that.

'Divorce is an impossibly hard transition in your life and he was there for a few months.'

Russell, however, wishes she had said that earlier. 'It would have been nice to hear [her] say that a few years earlier. A lot of the bad-boy thing and attendant pressures came from that time. Everything seeps out from that, and a mould grows over you, because of the implications. [However] it's really brave that she finally got around to talking about it in public ... the horse has bolted and life has moved on.'

Dennis Quaid said in 2004, 'I think Russell did Meg and I a big favour. He forced us to face up to something, because we were clinging on to a dead relationship.

'I felt hurt and humiliated, of course, but we hadn't been getting on for quite some time. We were bored with each other.'

Despite not regretting their relationship, the accusation

that Russell's relationship with Ryan was the cause for the underperforming box office still rankles.

Hackford told journalists, 'My biggest fear is that there's been so much exposure, people will think they've already seen this movie. And they haven't.'

His comments came after a reported early screening saw the crowd laugh during a kissing scene between the pair.

Russell felt compelled to reply to the insinuations about poor box-office returns. 'Just for clarity,' he said later, 'apart from a few kind of strange situations – mainly because of the conditions we were working in, 14,000ft up in the Andes where the weather patterns change every quarter of an hour – every day on that film was about the intensity of work, and Taylor didn't know I was in a relationship with Meg. It was only through people informing him during the course of interviews that he found out about it. Our personal relationship was separate to our working relationship. We went to work, we did the best job we possibly could for the director.'

Talking about the media's sudden fascination with him, he said to Tiscali, 'I have to try and keep a sense of humour about it all. Some of the things you read you get an immediate reaction to, so I've stopped reading things now. I do worry about my family though. Some people do try some nasty things to get at them and try to get a reaction from them. The important thing to me is that I'm not driven by people's praise and I'm not slowed down by people's criticism. I'm just trying to work at the highest level I can.'

CHAPTER SIXTEEN

RUSSELL'S CAREER ADDS UP

'Russell is very intense, very intense.'
– Ron Howard

When it was clear that Ron Howard's next project would be *A Beautiful Mind* (2001) – a biopic of John Nash, the Nobel Prize-winning mathematical genius who suffered from schizophrenia – the director began thinking about who would play the complex lead role. 'It was, on paper, a great screen performance, but kind of a scary character to take on. So I needed someone with real courage. John Nash is a very complex character and in interpreting that character you needed an actor with the ability, with the presence and charisma to command your interest over a period of time, and the talent to pull it off, also the nerve.

'When I met with him [Russell] I wasn't 100 per cent convinced going into the meeting, but I was very, very interested in discussing it with him. I found that his questions were important. The intelligence that he displayed in asking these questions was very exciting for me, because I knew he was charismatic, I knew he was talented. But I saw a level of intelligence that whoever played Nash had to be able to display. You can't really act it, fake it. It's not a matter of just saying the words. That spark has to be there, and I saw it there in spades.

'Russell is very intense, very intense. But I don't get the feeling it's a show. It's really about the vibe that he feels he needs to try to create something, or sometimes it's about the vibe he thinks the entire set needs to sort of get in the right space to maximise the scene.'

Howard went on to say, 'Russell is a very charismatic guy but a character actor at heart. He wants to discover a character, define it within his own terms, ingest it and then present it back to you in a way that's insightful and entertaining. This is kind of his genius.'

The director was keen to work with Russell but sought advice from other filmmakers. 'They said he really is an intense guy. But it's all about the work. If you're prepared and can debate his points, you won't have problems. It's not about being an egomaniac who wants things his way. He's challenging the material constructively.'

While Howard was keen to get Russell on board, it would take him and his producing partner Brian Grazer six months to convince him.

Grazer recalled, 'Sometimes you can deal with an actor's questions by saying, "This is what we're gonna do" and they jump on board. Russell is smart. He actually wanted to see the improvements – he didn't want to just hear about them. We had to produce them, show him several different drafts. Russell was in Austin with his band. Ron flew down there and Russell grilled him till five in the morning.'

Explaining what it was like with the actor, Howard said, 'Working with Russell is like filming on a small island. The weather's going to change every day, but it's where you want to be. He has a reputation for being dark or tense or stubborn, but he's not intractable. He is strongly opinionated and he doesn't suffer fools, but he doesn't have that almost pathological need to lay blame that some people do. At times he really digs his heels in because he feels that something important is at stake, but once you've gained his respect, he wants to be led. That's really having your cake and eating it too.'

Sylvia Nasar, whose biography of Nash is the source material for the film, said about Russell, 'What an inspired choice! Crowe isn't just beautiful. He's a superb actor who's got it all: emotional intensity, presence, brains. This is a drama about the mystery of the human mind in three acts: genius, madness, reawakening. Crowe will be totally convincing in all of Nash's incarnations. He'll convey Nash's raw mental power and confidence at the outset, his torment and terrible isolation during his illness, and finally, his incredibly moving triumph.'

Again Russell would be playing a real-life person.

Talking about the differences between Wigand and Nash, Russell noted, 'When Michael was talking about it as something he wanted me to create as opposed to copying, there wasn't a plan for me to meet him, but the more stuff I saw on him, the more I felt I couldn't get near him unless I tried to physically replicate him.

'So when I began to feel that I needed to wear his type of glasses and have hair like him, it felt more important to meet up. And I got some really good stuff out of that meeting, got some great insights.

'Nash as he is now is not a true witness to who he was as a younger man. We would ask questions like, "Did you ever smoke?" and he would say, "No" and yet we know he smoked for several years. "Did you ever wear a beard?" "Not that I can recall," and we have photographs of him in Europe wearing a beard. From that point on, we realised the movie would be based on broader aspects of his life.

'All I did ask was, "Would you like a cup of tea?" and he gave me such a complicated answer it was like "Whoa!"'

As before, Russell took getting into character seriously. 'With Nash, I wanted to find a couple of things that would help me. One was that I decided to grow my nails. He has long fingers and I thought if I grew my nails it would make me use my hands in a different way when I was writing on a blackboard, picking up paper.'

Maths wasn't Russell's strongest subject, however. 'I had a bit of a hiccup in the third year of high school. The

Above: Russell Crowe watches his team, the South Sydney Rabbitohs, as they warm up.

Below: Announcing a sponsorship deal between the Rabbitohs and Virgin Blue.

Above left: Russell Crowe was arrested for assault on 6 June, 2005.

Above right: The Pop-Up Book of Celebrity Meltdowns (Melcher Media, 2006) parodied the incident.

Below: Danielle Spencer and Russell arrive at Manhattan Criminal Court for a plea regarding Crowe's alleged assault.

Above: Russell's penthouse apartment in Sydney, Australia.

Below: Out and about in 2006 with his pregnant wife Danielle and son Charles.

Above: Russell Crowe starred alongside Christian Bale in *3:10 to Yuma* in 2007.

Below: At the film premiere for *3:10 to Yuma* on 21 August, 2007.

Above left: Out with his sons Charles and Tennyson in Beverly Hills, L.A.

Above right: Russell Crowe & The Ordinary Fear of God in concert in New York.

Below left: Danielle and Russell at the premiere of *American Gangster* in October, 2007.

Below right: At the *Body of Lies* premiere with Leonardo Di Caprio.

Russell and Dame Helen Mirren at the *State of Play* London premiere on 21 April, 2009.

One of the most highly anticipated films of 2010 is Ridley Scott's remake of *Robin Hood*, starring Russell Crowe in the title role.

Above: Russell leads the charge as Robin Hood.

Below: Practicing his sword fighting on the set of *Robin Hood* – but don't worry, he'll remember to remove those sunglasses before the cameras roll!

school I was at hired a non-English speaking Hungarian who was a professional of some great standing in Eastern Europe. But he hadn't learned the English language yet. He probably is a great asset to the teaching staff now, but we were his first class. That was when mathematics and I parted ways.

'The mathematics, at the moment, are so far beyond my understanding. It's about instinctively being able to find an answer to a very complicated question and then proving how you got to the answer. Thankfully it's only a movie because I was hopeless at maths when I was at school.'

What he was desperate to do, however, was show schizophrenia in a different light from other Hollywood films.

'I was tired of movies that were simply like going to the zoo when it came to mental health. You know that voyeuristic, "Ooh, that's what a crazy person's like." People always say crazy is without reason and I guarantee that's not true. So I made a more cohesive set of delusions to give the audience a hint of the experiment.'

Nash was a hard character to shake off. 'I had nightmares, lots of them,' Russell admitted. 'No matter what I'd done over the weekend, no matter how I'd tried to relax, 1 could not sleep the night before shooting. But I think that's part of the process – you delve into this stuff and you can't help but ask yourself how you'd feel in this situation.'

But it was all worth it. As Nasar said, 'The Nashes are

extremely happy with the movie, especially because, as Alicia [John's wife] put it, "We're going to have to live with it for a long time." Though Nash prefers action movies to dramas, he loved the humour and fast pace, and said, with evident pleasure, that he thought Russell Crowe looked a lot like him.'

The film was hit by accusations that the movie skirted over Nash's reported bisexuality. 'It's about taking an overview,' Russell said. 'And fine, so Sylvia Nasar raised the question of Nash's possible bisexuality. And certainly if you are that spectacularly unsuccessful with women, maybe it's just that they aren't for you. But we certainly hint at it. I mean, watch the movie – half the time I'm eyeing up other guys in the corridor. Besides, moviemaking is very Freudian. Any little gesture is a stone into a pond, mate. There's a future resonance at play here. So our level of sensitivity to the bisexual aspect should be applauded, not machine-gunned.'

Nasar waded into the debate, defending the film: 'It's nasty, but nobody's taking it seriously. Nash had several emotionally intense relationships with other men in his early twenties. In the homophobic, McCarthyite 1950s, that made him vulnerable. But he wasn't gay. Nobody who knew him thought he was gay. The biography never portrayed him as gay. A reporter from *USA Today* actually tried to tell that Ron Howard's not depicting Nash as a homosexual would be like Michael Mann making Muhammad Ali a 'white Hindu'. I felt like I was having an out-of-body experience. It was like the 1950s all over again when it was kosher to smear people by making allegations about their sexuality. Of course, people who read the book know otherwise.'

Russell was in a Berlin pub with the other cast and crew when he received the news that he had received an Oscar nomination for *A Beautiful Mind* – prompting Ron Howard to do a jig of joy at the news. However, the sight of the normally unassuming director dancing his heart out prompted Russell to say, 'On second thoughts, get down – you're a great director but you can't dance for shit!'

Howard said of the recognition, 'So to have the eight nominations, literally in every category in which we were candidates, it meant a lot to me as a director.'

'This is a powerful movie driven by a very challenging central character. None of us get nominated if Russell Crowe doesn't do the job he did in this movie.'

During the BAFTA awards, Russell made the headlines after TV producer Malcolm Gerrie cut the poem – *Sanctity* by Patrick Kavanagh – he read after accepting the Best Actor prize. It was a decision which would see him pinned to the wall by an irate Russell, with the words, 'You fucking piece, I'll make sure you never work in Hollywood,' ringing in his ear.

Gerrie was at the after-awards dinner at the Grosvenor House Hotel when the incident happened. He was talking to Sting when two of Russell's bodyguards approached him. He was taken to a room where Russell, enjoying a bottle of Victoria Bitter, was waiting for him and then proceeded to launch a series of insults at the startled man.

Russell's recollection of the night differed somewhat from what was reported. 'I had a conversation with the guy, and my question was "Are you responsible for cutting the speech?" and he said, "Yes." I told him what I thought about it. He was very dismissive about my opinion, so then I told him what I thought about it, plus some specificity. I never hit him – like some kind of gangland fucking bullshit, the way it was reported. I think the conversation took place just outside the kitchen.'

While it's not yet known if the TV director did take up the offer of a pint from a chastened or PR-directed Russell, it will no doubt be a dinner party conversation staple for years to come. For Russell, however, it was more bad publicity. The trouble was, it wasn't one of those things that could be waved over with a dismissive 'Oh, boys will be boys' gesture.

A hastily rearranged interview with *Empire* magazine only fuelled suggestions that he was trying to mend his bad boy image. The journalist's first interview had found Russell in a boisterous mood. The magazine noted that 'the meeting was a raucous, bawdy affair involving many tangents, literature, bisexuality, bottled water, tights – some 157 swear words.

'A few days later Russell Crowe contacted *Empire*, via

his publicist, to express reservations. He had apparently undergone something of a change of heart. Didn't think he'd given a good account of himself. Wasn't happy. And, in turn, requested a second interview, to restore what he considered to be a much needed sense of balance.'

Incidents like the BAFTA one and reports of barroom brawling late at night were seized upon by the media. A backlash was beginning and he was giving them as much ammunition as they would need. It has even been suggested that is the reason why he lost out on a second Oscar. However, his most notorious moment would come during his next movie. And appropriately it would be a film about fighting.

CHAPTER SEVENTEEN

RUSSELL'S REPUTATION TAKES A BATTERING

'I had probably 12 mild concussions. If you're going to make a movie about a boxer, you're going to get hit.'

– Russell Crowe

For Russell *Cinderella Man* started in 1997, when he first read the script. He fell in love with it almost immediately but his status wasn't quite high enough, in the industry's mind, and so off it sailed into the laps of other actors – like Ben Affleck – who were being courted to play the part of boxer Jim Braddock.

Directors such as Penny Marshall, Billy Bob Thornton and Lasse Hallstrom all circled around the project, but still it didn't get made. And there was Russell, still hanging around, desperate to get his chance at it. Harvey Weinstein, he decided, was the best man to make the film happen. The fiery, perfectionist actor and the no-nonsense studio boss seemed like a volatile team-up, and one that was about as combustible as you could get in Hollywood.

The pair had previous history, too. Russell had been earmarked to play the Bard in the Weinstein's company's Oscar-winning smash *Shakespeare in Love*. However, he had a problem with the script – a problem that only he seemed to have – and so he refused the role.

'I was fucking right about that movie, too,' he said. 'It was a 100 per cent fucking home run, except the central character of William Shakespeare was not a fucking writer. He was not smelly enough, he was not unshaven enough, and obviously hadn't had enough to drink. He was some prissy pretty boy. What the fuck? That's so disrespectful.'

However, his chance to make amends with Weinstein nearly fell through after Russell had to turn down their meeting. 'He called me at about quarter to nine in the morning and wanted me to magically turn up for a meeting at 12 o'clock in Tribeca, but I was doing press around Central Park. I was, "Look, mate, can't do it." So he told me to get fucked. I rang my agent and said, "Hey, Harvey just told me to get fucked before 9am." He goes, "Oh, my God, what do you think that means?" I said, "I think it means we're getting somewhere."'

Armed with the project Russell went to *A Beautiful Mind* director Ron Howard. *Cinderella Man* would let the director tackle another genre in a diverse film-making career that had included action, drama, family and blockbuster. Yet making a sports film concerned him. 'I worried about trying to find a way to execute the boxing in a way that was really exciting and truthful for fight fans.

'I knew I would do all the research; I would try to find every good camera angle. At the end of the day I felt challenged by it, until I realised I was really over-thinking it. A great actor who I had already worked with, Russell Crowe, was going to be playing Braddock. We have a great creative collaboration going on. If Russell thinks he can do something, and says he can do something, he will, by God, deliver.'

Talking about teaming up with Howard again, Russell said, 'We have a lot in common, but we're also very different in a lot of ways. Ron's a very smart man and a lot more complex and interesting than people think he is. He's a strong leader and I respect him a lot.'

To get into shape Russell decided to cut out the alcohol. 'I'm preparing for my role in *The Cinderella Man* so I'm getting into shape and alcohol tends to put weight on.'

It was a rigorous routine – even more so because of Russell's obsession with striving for authenticity. 'It was very physically demanding. The training was difficult because Jim was a heavyweight boxer back in the time of The Great Depression and the fighters weren't nearly as big as they are today. I adopted the same training methods that Jim Braddock would've used when he was fighting.

'The film was shot in Toronto, Canada and I met some great young boxers who were members of the Canadian boxing team. I trained with them and I even brought some of them over to my farm in Australia to train.'

However, Russell had to undergo physiotherapy after he dislocated his shoulder in a sparring match. 'After two months of training and preparation, it was actually the first time I got into the ring to do some sparring, can you believe that? I knew instantly. I felt it go in the second round.'

'It was the hardest training I've ever done, and I'm over 40 now, so it was probably the wrong time to start,' Crowe added. 'There's a lot of old war wounds that came back.'

But the two months of physiotherapy proved a blessing in disguise, according to Russell. 'By the end of week three we did ten rounds on the hand mitts. I was sparring again by the end of week four. Frankly, because of the injury it extended the time we had to prepare, and the skill level, the body, the choreography, everything moved forward. Everything was given more space and as a result everything was more successful.'

Howard added, 'We decided this would have more contact than most boxing movies. I thought if I can just take the audience into the ring with him, and let the audience experience those fights, not from a distance, but as much as possible right in there as though they were alongside Braddock in a way.'

In fact, Russell insists all the pain was worth it because it showed the story of Braddock to a wider world. 'It was terrible. Doctors told me I was crazy for going through with this film, but I couldn't stop. I really couldn't. I trained for at least 10 hours a day and my doctor told me that I was tearing up my muscle tissue.

'I just couldn't not make this film. There was a whole crew waiting and I just couldn't stop the film from being made. I was the one that took the script to Ron Howard and convinced Renée Zellweger to play my wife in the film, so I felt a responsibility to see the project through to completion.'

Because of the sheer logistics of boxing on screen, the actors would be hit for real. The film's on-set doctor believed that the actor took such a battering that he feared multiple concussions. The film's boxing consultant Angelo Dundee said, 'If a fighter had the injury like he had, he wouldn't fight for six months.'

Talking about Russell, Dundee, who was Muhammad Ali's trainer, said, 'I'm tellin' ya, the kid has a great left hook. He could have been a fighter, sure he could. He loves boxing.'

Russell said of working with Dundee, 'For me to have the advantage of Angelo's mind, it was a joy. All the pain and stuff goes away because there is amusement and education going on and there's a transference of knowledge that was really generous of him.

'He built me to do all the things that he wanted me to do. I'm facing guys who were Commonwealth Games gold medalists.

'Man, I'm not silly. I wouldn't go anywhere near those sort of blokes in a different situation. But Angelo built in me the ability and then, in his parlance, just opened them up like a can of tomatoes.'

Russell had originally asked former heavyweight fighter Joe Bugner to be the film's consultant. 'I told Russell that pro boxing is a very dangerous business,' Bugner said at the time. 'Even in the sparring sessions we'll be doing, when we're all padded up, he'll have to concentrate hard on what's going on or he can get hurt.

'After six weeks in the ring with me, he will come out of this knowing a lot more about how to handle himself in a fight.'

Russell decided to go with Dundee instead, but when Russell got injured, Bugner criticised Dundee's training methods. Bugner revealed that Russell promptly phoned him up and insulted him in a manner for which Bugner will 'never, ever forgive him'.

He told the *Sydney Daily Telegraph*, 'He started at me, calling me an idiot and saying that I didn't know anything about boxing. I said to him, "Let me tell you something. I've been in boxing for 33 years. I know more about boxing than you'll ever know about acting. I'm not a phony, whereas all you do is read scripts."

'I said, "Russell, go and shove your head up your ass." And I hung up. The guy's 40 going on 12. I was never going to put up with his silly tantrums. He behaves like a fucking girl.

'If I saw him, I wouldn't give him the time of day. If he approached me, I would stand and wait. I would be right there in front of the bloke. And I would have to resort to my old career.'

Angelo, however, said of working with Russell, 'It went really well. Russell is a nice, easy human being and a great athlete. He runs and rides mountain bike up in the mountains in Australia. He has a nice big ranch with an Olympic swimming pool.'

Talking about working with Russell, Renée Zellweger said, 'He finds it fun to dissect material and learn about it and live it and tell a story from the inside. So I knew that we would be compatible in the way that we approach the work.'

Asked whether he gave her a hard time, she said, 'He absolutely did.'

Zellweger would clarify her comments, explaining, 'Russell is very serious about the way that he approaches his work and the way that his characters come to life, and his level of commitment, in terms of how far he's willing to go to realise a character.

'Creatively, it's so much more satisfying to work with someone like Russell, who really wants it to be honest and he wants the integrity of the project to be maintained throughout.

'He is so kind and so understanding of everybody else's position, and it's just such a gift.'

Paul Giamatti, who played Braddock's manager Joe Gould, told *Rolling Stone* magazine, 'The first thing he said was, "I can just be a horrible, irascible guy, and I apologise ahead of time if I get that way." I had heard horror stories, but I loved working with him.'

He would add to darkhorizons.com, 'He's a super-complicated guy, but really smart. I had more fun working with him than anybody I think I have ever worked with. I play his trainer, so everything I did was with him and I kind of loved him, even though there was a lot about him that I can't even begin to understand and he's a dangerously complicated guy! But from an acting point of view, if you walk in the room and start throwing stuff at him, he just loves it, because he seems to me like he is only really truly happy when he's acting.'

However, Fulvio Ceceres, who played referee McAvoy, has admitted that there are difficulties in working with him. 'Russell is a bit of a mystery and enigma. He can be the most generous and gregarious person ever and then there can be days that you don't want to bother him.

'I don't profess to know him that well but I'd have to say that overall my experiences with him have been great. I do know that he is one of the best actors I've ever worked with and I believe that he is one of the best actors of our generation.'

Another actor in the film, Craig Bierko (who played boxer Max Baer), told journalists that despite working with Russell for a month, 'I don't know him from Adam. There was literally not a single moment where I felt like we were actually bonding, or having a conversation.'

As reported on WENN.com, Crowe hit back, blasting,

'Craig Bierko has an imagination. His recollection of the experience is significantly different from anyone else's.

'I spent my 40th birthday party on a satellite connection with my wife and child in Australia. Sorry I didn't invite Craig. I didn't think it was relevant.

'The fact is, he hadn't done enough work and he had to be drilled and drilled, and brought up to where we needed him to be – because if Max Baer isn't frightening and isn't capable, then we don't have much of a movie.

'Craig has never been in this kind of situation before. It has never been required of him to put this much work and this much of himself into a role.

'He didn't realise what he was getting into... He realised afterwards.'

Paddy Considine, who played Mike Wilson, said, 'That man is extraordinary. That actor is just extraordinary! If you can't listen to him, you can't listen to anybody.

'First we shot the scene on Russell Crowe about six o'clock in the evening and then, instead of turning around right on to me, we did the whole sequence of the pens being put on the table, which took hours. It was shot from every conceivable angle. Every different actor who brought a pen had to be shot. It was shot from overhead. Here and there. And this is a day that began at six o'clock that morning. So, finally, they brought the camera around to me at almost midnight and I was thinking, "I don't know how to do this now. I can't do it. I'm tired. I've forgotten completely what Russell said."

'But Russell sat off-camera and played the scene as fully as he'd played it six hours before. It was incredible. I've never seen an actor do that. So all I had to do is hang out, do you know what I mean? And respond to him. I was thinking, "How can I do this!? How can I do this!?" and in effect, he did it for me. He's very compelling to listen to.'

Cinderella Man wasn't the box office hit that Howard and Russell were hoping for, despite AMC Theatres in America taking the unprecedented step of promising a full refund to cinemagoers if they weren't impressed with the film. Only 100 people asked for their money back.

A cinema spokesperson said, 'The whole effort was to focus attention on what is a beautiful film that deserves an audience but just hasn't got one. It's in competition with films with lots of special effects and big action this summer. This is a quiet film.'

Talking about the exhibitors' decision, Russell said, 'Well, to me, that was the exhibitors just not quite believing what was in front of their eyes, that this film they thought was a good movie wasn't getting the audience it deserved. And they see everything, it's their job – they screen movies.

'And you're talking about a movie that in test screenings got 94 or 95 per cent audience reactions in the two top boxes: "Love the movie" and "Definitely recommend it". So theatres were just saying to people,

"We're guaranteeing that this is a great movie. Come and see it and we'll give you your money back if you don't like it." I saw it as an incredibly positive thing and so did Ron. It's his best movie and he's made some great films.'

Ultimately, however, Russell was disappointed by the box office showing. 'It's a fucking prick of a job, you know? Particularly when you get successful with it. People don't understand why your life suddenly changed when, hey, to them it's fucking ten bucks at the movies, it's over in a couple of hours. They don't understand the prep, they don't understand the real physical shit that you put yourself through. I mean, the last movie's an example – shoulder surgery part way through preparation.

'And it's a $100 million train, man, and I'm the fucking guy that drives the train. And I've got to get back on that train and make sure that this thing is completed. And not everybody takes the same attitude towards it. Not everybody takes it seriously, you know. If it's not going to be that serious, I don't want to do it. It's a personal taste. I don't like watching an actor have the same fucking hairdo from time period to time period, from character to character – I just think it's bullshit. It's a waste of money and a waste of my time as an audience member.'

Russell would be making headlines for all the wrong reasons again – this time he was accused of hurtling a phone at a hotel clerk. Russell claimed that, frustrated with constantly asking for his phone in his room to be fixed and put off by the attitude of the clerk on duty, he went down to complain in person.

His publicist, Robin Baum, told *Extra*, 'Words were exchanged and Crowe wound up throwing the phone against the wall. He regrets that he lost his temper, but at no time did he assault anyone or touch any hotel employee.'

His lawyer, Gerald Lefcourt said, 'This arose because he was trying to get his wife on the phone in Australia. He was in his room. He couldn't get a line and there was a disagreement.'

Russell was arrested and was arraigned on charges of second-degree assault and fourth-degree criminal possession of a weapon. Despite assistant District Attorney asking for bail to be set at $5,000, Russell was released on his own recognisance. He called the hotel incident the 'most shameful situation I've ever gotten myself in.'

His *Cinderella Man* co-star, Giamatti added, 'He's a complicated guy. I didn't have to fight him for Alpha Male supremacy. He does do that and he's the first person to admit that he does it. But for some reason he was great with me and I ended up kind of loving him, because he's amazing to work with. He's a very kind guy, but he's a very complicated guy. A lot of stuff gets blown out of proportion. I saw things happen that when I read about them in the paper they had no relation to what I saw happen. He gets a bit of a bum rap. He's complicated and there are people he wants to pull the Alpha male thing with – why I don't know. But I didn't have to. I think maybe he took pity on me, because he realised I was the Zeta male.'

Talking to David Letterman soon after the incident, Russell said, 'I was in Manchester, England. I flew there on Friday and I flew back to New York on Sunday. I've just got to cut myself some slack.

'I'm just getting used to being a husband and a father away from home and that's a level of abject loneliness I'm just not used to at all.

'As my wife says, that's not really much of an excuse because millions of fathers and husbands travel for business all the time. I'm just new at it. Actually, quite frankly, I hope I never get used to it. I don't want to be away from my family like this.'

In an interview before the incident, he did say, 'I can't wait to see them. I don't mean to wish the days away, but the day of their arrival cannot come too soon for me. I'm more than a little lonely but trying to fill the void with work to distract myself. My wife is a blessing, my son a gift from God. I don't know what I have ever done to deserve such good fortune.'

For the police officers involved it was a surreal experience to arrest a Hollywood movie star – and it got even more surreal. 'I got a little bit claustrophobic at one point,' Russell recalled. 'Quite frankly, it was not an enjoyable experience at all, but I went up to the bars of the cell at one point and asked the arresting officer if she would like me to sing her a song.

'She goes, "That'll be a first." So, in order to relax myself, I sang an old Irish folk tune to her.' The song in question was rather appropriately entitled, 'I'm A Man You Don't Meet Every Day'.

Russell was taken to get his mug shot, and as he stood there bewildered by what was happening, the officer who took his mug shot told him, 'Put your jewellery away, it makes you look like a Hispanic gangsta' and 'Don't smile so much, buddy.'

In a bizarre twist of fate, the same person that took his mug shot would later turn up during the filming of *American Gangster*. Russell remembered, 'Oddly, right at the beginning of the shoot, there was a guy walking around the set a lot that I just thought I recognised from somewhere.

'He came over on about the third or fourth day and he said, "Hi, I'm Scotty. I'm the police advisor on the movie." I said, "Great, cool, we'll have a bit of a chat later on..." And he said, "No, no – I, uh, you know that night you had your problem? I took your mug shot!"'

Russell's close friend Nicole Kidman defended him, saying, 'Obviously, I heard what happened and I'm a very good friend of his – one of his best friends, I would say. So you're there for your best friends.'

Russell was stunned by the media's reaction. 'Travelling businessmen get touchy or testy with hotel staff in every major city all around the world. That doesn't excuse the fact that I lost my temper ... what I did was stupid. I admitted that straight away. I got a $160 court cost fine for something that would have had more news print about it than some very horrific and specific things that we should know about in our community. That is what I mean by getting it into perspective.'

Soon afterwards, more stories of his diva behaviour began to be reported by the press. One such story accused him of hiring a person to light his cigarettes for him during work on *Cinderella Man*. But, Giamatti explained, 'He had boxing gloves on the whole time and he smokes a lot, and his wardrobe guy was sticking cigarettes in his mouth and lighting them. Somehow it became this whole thing about how he had this lackey who had to light his cigarettes for him. That's not what it was.'

It also didn't help that Russell began a war of words with Joan Rivers. She said, 'Usually the bigger the star, the nicer they are. It's the ones with a few hits that act like they're special and they're so not. Russell Crowe is so rude. I have no time for him at all. He's only sexy in his head. He's so arrogant. Why would he want to go to bed with anyone but himself?'

Russell hit back, saying, 'Joan Rivers was calling me an evil son of a bitch. As far as I know, I've passed her in a corridor, once. Is it maybe just because I've never done one of her puerile fucking red carpet conversations where we talk about what you're fucking wearing or what your date is wearing? I don't give a fuck what my hairdo is like. You know, all of these things that supposedly add up to some great gap in my construction as a man, I couldn't give a shit.'

Despite opening with an impressive $18 million at the US box office, *Cinderella Man* struggled to keep up that momentum, with some media critics arguing that the phone-throwing incident had hurt his reputation. 'Crowe has single-handedly turned *Cinderella Man* into a financial disappointment,' said showbiz columnist Jeffrey Wells. 'His ability to demand the big bucks may be in great peril [if] audiences are going to look at his films ... and say, "Screw it, I don't want to pay to see that thug."'

The movie was also released in the summer, competing with films like *Batman Begins*.

'We got taught a lesson about that,' said Russell. 'Brian Grazer and Ron Howard said right from the beginning that we had to wait with this movie. But Universal were so buoyed by the reactions to the early screenings that they were really bullish: "We'll carve out a piece of the summer with this movie because people love it." And then it comes down to the differences in the American cinema seasons. We didn't have any capes or hi-tech equipment or utility belts – we just had a bloke in a pair of shorts.'

CHAPTER EIGHTEEN

CROWE TAKES COMMAND

'At times I will go into a very dark place. Don't get sucked into my vortex when that happens.'

– Russell Crowe

Patrick O'Brian's novels about the British naval hero Captain Jack Aubrey were hugely popular, so it wasn't surprising that Hollywood tried to sail the series onto the big screen. Charlton Heston was O'Brian's first choice when talk of a movie started in 1995, but by the time Peter Weir had joined the production years later, times had moved on.

Tom Rothman, the Twentieth Century Fox chairman, asked, 'Who today is "Lucky" Jack Aubrey? There was only one name on the list.'

'Russell Crowe was always my first choice to play Jack Aubrey,' said Weir. 'Russell had that natural energy and authority and he took command of that ship from the beginning.'

Russell, however, had his doubts after reading the

script, as Weir recalled. 'Russell's firsts words to me were, "This character, there must be more to him than what's in this script or the book." I said to him, "It's true. But it's not on the page. Aubrey is a little limited. What you see is what you get." In my experience, when you have a less than full character, it's the casting that is the secret.'

Some fans of the books were critical of casting Russell as Jack Aubrey and Paul Bettany as Aubrey's confidant, Dr Stephen Maturin. Not because of their talents but because in the book Aubrey's weight at its highest is 17 stone, while Maturin is stick thin. While Russell would bulk up, he was never going to get that big.

Weir defended his decision to cast Russell and Bettany, saying, 'There was the danger, physically, of Stephen and Jack looking like Laurel and Hardy, such is their disparity in appearance in the novels. When casting I ended up with people who accurately fitted the physical description, and that left them open to parody. Paul didn't fit that description, but his reading was so impressive that it led me to think I would share a long voyage with Paul.'

One obvious benefit of casting Bettany alongside Russell was that they had experience of working together.

'Paul and I developed a kind of creative shorthand in *A Beautiful Mind* that I thought would serve us well in establishing the Jack-Stephen dynamic. I was glad that Peter cast Paul. With another person, you might actually have had to break down a scene and explain it. Paul and I were able to get to a point of depth that you might have to work ten times harder with somebody else to even touch on,' said Russell.

On paper at least, Weir himself was an odd choice to bring the books to the big screen. He told *Empire*, 'Action is a new route for me. And Patrick O'Brian's prose is dauntingly magnificent. When I first shook the books and the prose fell out on the desk, I must admit I had a moment of doubt: you have to replace that with imagery. But I've always had an interest in the historical fiction of this period and would look forward to the next instalment from O'Brian, when he was alive, like people would with film-makers they admire.'

A huge fan of the books, Weir had turned down the chance to helm the movies twice when the rights were in the hands of Sam Goldwyn and Disney respectively. However, he agreed to make the movie with Twentieth Century Fox – with Universal and Miramax co-producing – because he could make it less about how Jack and Stephen first met and more about the journey.

'I said if I was to do one of O'Brian's books, I'd want it to be about the ship and a mission, not when the characters first meet. A film of the first novel was in danger of lending itself to parody. Two friends meeting, one's a spy, the other's having an affair with an admiral's wife... all very rollicking but it's too tongue and cheek.

'My favourite O'Brian stories are when it's a long journey, and in particular the middle to later section of *Far Side of the World*. And that's what I offered as a script. I could only focus on that part and had to omit all of Maturin's espionage.'

Weir also explained why they used the name from the first book – *Master and Commander* – when most of the film is based on the tenth instalment *Far Side of the World*. 'I never agreed with the decision to use *Master and Commander*. I wanted to call it *Far Side of the World*. But the studios found the title tested effectively. People liked the idea of Russell Crowe as *Master and Commander*. *Far Side of the World* sounded too arty.'

For several days Russell visited Dorset, where Aubrey hailed from, in a bid to get the accent right – only to be told by a linguist that a Dorset man in the 18th century would have sounded Australian!

Asked about his character, he said, 'I loved the image that Peter put in my head when we talked about this man – a sailor with calluses on his hands, who has grown up in the navy and knows every part of his ship. If the sails aren't going up fast enough, he will jump down and grab the rope and see what is causing the problem. And those same callused, thickened hands then pick up this delicate feminine instrument, the violin, and he will play from his heart the things he can never say.'

Weir added, 'When we initially talked, I explained that I usually like to work from a sense of joie de vivre on the set, a reckless energy. After Russell heard me out, he said, "That's fine, but at times I will go into a very dark place. Don't get sucked into my vortex when that happens."

'I saw that a couple of times and it was kind of alarming – very brooding, very hard to talk to on those days. Russell was inside this impenetrable black hole where he draws great inspiration, because the work that comes out of some of these dark spots is quite stunning. He's searching for something and he has to do it alone. You can't help him.'

Because of Russell's childhood fear of the ocean – after he was stranded at sea when his boat ran out of fuel – he was somewhat hesitant about setting sail again.

'Before I made this movie I wasn't comfortable in the water. The one big ocean trip I'd done was when I was 15 years old. We went from Sydney to Auckland on a Russian cruise ship. Now calling it a cruise ship is really generous. We hit 22-foot swells the first day, and in no time it smelled like a hospital ship during the First World War. There was vomit all over the floor, and every sharp corner had blood dripping off it from where the passengers had been heaved into it. So my experiences with the deep ocean have not been positive.

'That was my dirty little secret. I knew I was bad on water and had to overcome it.'

In another interview, he added, 'At first I was using travel sickness pills, but you can't be taking pills and doing lines on camera.

'I've always thought that I was not very good on boats. So it was time to try and see if it was not a psychosis but something that could be addressed physically, by actually doing miles in the water.'

One of the film's technical consultants, Andrew Reay-Ellers, said, 'To get a closer look at the workings of the rigging I gave him a quick safety orientation and we climbed aloft. Just before we went up I admitted I was a bit nervous about it and said, "If I manage to get you hurt I'll be out of a job." Russell paused, looked at me with a wry smile and said, "Mate, if you get me hurt we're ALL out of a job..." As if this weren't enough, once we were aloft I looked down and there was [executive producer] Duncan Henderson watching us intently. I found out later that Russell going aloft was something that I should have "cleared" first.

'Throughout the filming a number of scenes required him to be up in the rig, and he did every bit of that climbing and those stunts himself. You'll see a scene in the movie filmed from a helicopter where Russell and James D'Arcy are both at the top of the mainmast above the topgallants. It's easy to see that it really is them, and that there would have been no easy way to fake that shot.'

Russell would recall his experience filming those shots, saying, 'The character I was playing had no problems with this stuff. So I had no problems with it, if I just allowed myself to play the character. James D'Arcy really wasn't into the idea of climbing to the top of the mast, so they were going to build it on a soundstage and shoot it against a blue screen. I said to James, "Well, that just cheapens the shot. Look, I'm scared of heights too, and I understand it's dangerous. But I'm gonna do this. I'm gonna do it without a safety rope so if I do fall, it's good night Irene. But I've been working my body enough to know that I'm capable of doing things that Jack is capable of doing."

'James looked up at the swaying mast, 157 feet above the water and six-foot swells, and did it. When we got down he asked me, "How can you do that if you don't like doing it?" I said, "That's not the way you've got to approach it. You can't fucking wrap yourself in cotton because you're an important entertainer. You're only entertaining people if you are servicing the character."'

Armed with several books on nautical life, including a copy of *Sailing for Dummies* that Jodie Foster sent to him, Russell was determined to make sure he had his sea legs.

'I hooked up with a vessel called the MV *Surprise* in Fiji, which is owned by a fella called Mark Johnson. He's also an obsessive Patrick O'Brian fan. We went 270 nautical miles south-southwest of Fiji to a place called Conway's Reef. That is when you truly understand the might and power of the ocean, when the weather is up and there are eight or ten-foot swells. By the time I got to the film set, I found that physically I was fine.

'I was probably one of the dozen people in the whole cast and crew who didn't throw up. But I thought it would damage the credibility of the character if the midshipmen witnessed their captain hurling over the side of the ship.'

Russell also learnt how to play violin. After reading that his character was a proficient violinist, Russell got in touch with violinist Richard Tognetti. 'I said to myself, "You're not allowed to pretend that you're a violinist." Richard is the director of the Australian Chamber Orchestra and we've become friends, so I asked him to be my violin teacher. It was a very long process and very strange things happened. I used to put my violin down after 45 minutes of rehearsing and I'd feel very lightheaded and euphoric. I thought that's amazing that it makes you feel like this."

'Then I realised that I wasn't breathing while I was playing. I started getting really bad sore throats, so I came up with this system where I would hold a bit of rock candy between my teeth so at least it kept saliva going down the back of my throat, and I taught myself to breathe with the playing, as if I was singing. I can't say I claimed the instrument but I was OK.'

Talking about his research process, he added, 'If you give me a script I'll be ready to act in the morning. But if you have the time, I love going through the process of investigation and discovery. I'm a history buff, and that's the fun part of the job.'

Russell would spend hours in make-up applying all the scars over his body that Aubrey could conceivably have – although most were never seen on screen.

Once again he was acting as leader of men on set, and once again he would make sure everyone knew who was the boss. 'I got every man in the cast three shirts – different colours, depending on what rank they were on the ship. I gave them name tags, a length of thread and a needle. They had 12 hours to report back in uniform with a name tag sewn on.

'It wasn't for my ego. I just felt the experience would be bigger and better if we all allowed ourselves to play the game. There were a couple who did a sloppy job. They were talked to.'

Terry Dolan, who played Mr Lamb in the movie, said, 'I could never completely express what it was like to work with Russell. That will always only be felt in my heart. I will say that I personally found him as a man, intuitive, directed, dedicated, generous to a fault! Gentle, kind, observant, diligent and intelligent. As an actor, all of the above and more. I saw him do things on set to help people that mostly went unnoticed by others.'

Giving an example, he added to maximumcrowe.net, 'During one scene when we ran the rehearsal for camera a couple of times, a fellow cast member was a little concerned that by the time he arrived on the deck from below, the camera and Russell [would be] gone. We were discussing this and I noticed Russell, whilst talking to someone else, listening. I tried to reassure the cast member that it'd be OK and I'd try to help him into the camera shot earlier. However, as the camera went for the take, Russell slowed as he got to us and stopped for longer than he had been. And as the cast member reached the deck, and thus camera shot, [Russell] moved away. He had done this on purpose, in my view, and thus allowed this cast member to share in his camera shot. Not something he had to do, and he never spoke of it to that cast member or anyone else. Very gracious. But I spotted it!

'We ate together, drank together, played rugby together, watched the World Cup and Australian rugby and football together. We went to water parks together and played music together, watched movies together, too. So much stuff I can't remember [it] all, I'm sure. We acted like a crew and he the captain.'

Reay-Ellers added, 'He seemed to want us all to "become" the fictional crew. He definitely seems to enjoy the camaraderie of a whole team working together. He really started to inhabit the role of captain, and many of the extras always referred to him that way. During pre-production he got the cast and extras shirts whose colours designated their character's rank, and monogrammed name tags which he asked everyone to sew on themselves. He was sort of giving everyone a bonding experience, and also testing people to see who was in the spirit of the project and who was conscientious and professional about any job they tackled.'

Bettany said of working with Russell again, 'We are good mates, and it's nice when we get to work together because we see a lot of each other. We work well together. If you trust people you're working with, it's easier to be more risky.

'Russell goofs around a lot of the time, but he takes his job seriously.

'Russell speaks his mind, and lots of people pay money to see that. If you took away Russell speaking his mind, you take away what Russell is.'

Fans of the book weren't happy with some of the changes to the story – in particular that the enemy frigate is French, whereas historically it was American. Historian Count Nikolai Tolstoy, stepson and biographer of O'Brian, said, 'Generally it is faithful to the book apart from this glaring exception. Even several of the Americans involved are embarrassed about it. I hope people who see the film will then enjoy the proper version of the story by reading the book.'

However, Weir defended the decision. 'Of course, I was aware of what a joke it would be making what is an American movie about chasing an American ship, although that might have been interesting – but it was more about the 1812 war aspect. That was a dirty, nasty war that would never be comprehended by people who hadn't read about it. What is much more interesting is around the year of 1805, when Napoleon was so successful in Europe prior to Trafalgar.'

Talking about the chances of doing a sequel, Russell told the *Tribune*, 'The possibility of doing another one was in my mind from the beginning. These are interesting enough characters to sustain many stories. After all, O'Brian wrote 20 of these books.

'But it's purely an economic question. It's very expensive to make a film set in this time period. So if we're only to get one shot at it, we wanted to get it right.'

And the costume certainly had an effect on Danielle. Russell said, 'My wife wants me to make *Master and Commander 2* – she kinda liked that costume.'

Another person who wanted a sequel was actor Billy Boyd, who played coxswain Barnett Bondon in the film. Talking to HollywoodNews.com, he said, 'There are 21 books of *Master and Commander*, and Fox already own the ship, so a lot of people, I think, were confused as to why there hasn't been a sequel yet. We'll just have to wait and see.

'Peter said that I won't die in the next one, but he said I will die in the third one. So I've still got another movie, and then I've got a death scene. So, great. I do hope they make some more as I had great fun making that film.'

However, Weir said in 2005, 'No, I think it's most unlikely. I think that while it did well-ish at the box office, it didn't generate that kind of monstrous, rapid income that provokes a sequel.'

CHAPTER NINETEEN

A GOOD YEAR FOR RUSSELL

'I love to work quickly, and he does as well. We keep it fresh.'

– Ridley Scott

Russell and Scott's decision to make the first movie they made together after *Gladiator* a romantic comedy was something of a perverse one – especially in Russell's mind.

'The fact that Ridley and I would get together again and do a low-budget comedy, instead of what people expect – a $150 million blood fest – I enjoyed that part of it. I do the stuff that I have some kind of emotional connection to. All I'm trying to do when I do my job is not be elevated in your mind ... if you're in the cinema and you have an emotional connection to the film, then that's a simple reason for me to do my job. The reality is I just want to tell a story that's gonna touch you. But it's just a story. It's not going to change the world, it's not going to change bad political policy.'

Talking about his character – 'an English banker who

is an absolute arsehole', Russell said to *Film Review*, 'Uncle Harry taught him the difference between a good and bad red wine, the difference between a good and bad cigar and the importance of a blue suit. Unfortunately he taught him all of that around the age of 11! All the things his uncle put inside him as a young man are still there – they've just been reconfigured by life.

'There is a saying in Provence: "You don't own the chateau. The chateau owns you." We're basing the change in his life on that reconfiguration that happens, so all the things his uncle teaches him add up to something completely different than the way they've added up in his life. He goes back to the source of that knowledge and his life is changed and revitalised and he becomes a different sum of those parts.

'This is a film that basically says people never die as long as you keep them in your heart.'

Russell agreed to do *A Good Year* after witnessing Scott's sniffy manner towards the French people. 'Ridley has had a house in Provence for the last 15 years, therefore the story of the Anglo-Franco dynamic is something that he knows absolutely.

'In talking to Ridley he will casually abuse French people without even being consciously aware that he's doing it in an English manner, just as my French friends will casually abuse the English in the same way. As an outsider and a New Zealander born in Australia this to me was very funny. I wanted to examine that dynamic because this is two countries that share so much more common ground than they'll care to admit.

'Yes, there's a different language but there's a sensibility and an understanding of life in both countries that is very similar, though neither would ever admit that. There's been many times they've been each other's strongest and closest ally.'

Russell and Scott's exhausting work ethic hardly helped bridge the gaps, though, with Russell claiming, 'Oh, the French crew were a little perturbed by Ridley and me because we tend to work at a certain speed, and have a "The day has started, let's get into it" sort of attitude, you know? And I think after the first five days of shooting, the crew representative talked to the producer and said, "If these guys keep working at this pace, they're going to kill us!"

'We hadn't really noticed that everybody was starting to freak out, that 45 to 50 set-ups a day wasn't their normal pace. We had a great relationship with the crew eventually, it just took a little understanding.

Another reason was that his character's love of wine aped Russell's yearning for it too. He is a big appreciator of fine wine, with thousands of carefully vetted bottles housed in his ranch. Not surprising really for a man who grew up in a family that had a catering business and owned pubs.

Russell remembers one encounter where his expertise was needed, when he and *Gladiator* co-star Connie

Nielsen went for a meal at a top restaurant in London to celebrate the beginning of the filming of the Roman epic. They decided to splash out on a wine that was made in the same year they were born. 'This particular wine was Australian and, when it was opened and brought to the table, you could smell from two feet away that it was corked,' Russell recollected. Forty-five minutes later, the waiter finally relented.

The film was a reunion for him and Ridley Scott. Not that Ridley hadn't wanted his leading man to star in some of the other films he had directed. 'He asked me to do *Black Hawk Down* but I had just done a movie where there was a helicopter in the background (*Proof of Life*) and I wasn't interested. Then he wanted me to do *Kingdom of Heaven*, but I was in the middle of doing something else and said, "You'll have to wait a year," and he was like, "Well, screw you!"'

'We're really heavily connected now,' Russell said in another interview. 'We have a connection in aesthetics. We have a connection in work ethic. We have a connection in our senses of humour. He knows the thing that no one gets in articles: I'm a great lieutenant. I work for the boss.'

Scott said of his leading man, 'The Cary Grant character is hard to find today. Not too many actors can actually pull that off. The original Cary Grant was remarkable in that that's who he was. Although he did comedy, he was always trying to play drama, and no one would let him. And thank God. Russell crosses that border because he can do anything.'

It must have irked the actor to hear countless questions about swapping drama for a comedy. 'If somebody is familiar with all the films that I've done, then they know there's a gay, football-playing plumber in *The Sum of Us* and there's the ice-skating sheriff in *Mystery, Alaska.* Comedy is not a place that I haven't been to – it's probably a full third of all the films that I've done.'

The film has more than a whiff of summer holiday about it – an accusation that was hardly denied by its cast members. 'It's just playing silly buggers with your old mate for 12 weeks in Provence. I mean, that's a hell of a good gig, that.'

French critics were quick to slam the film for reinforcing rural French stereotypes. 'Appalling from start to finish, *A Good Year* collapses under clichés of an ochre Luberon made for a loaded Anglo-Saxon elite,' sneered *Liberation*.

Even Rupert Murdoch blasted the film, calling it flop during a shareholders meeting. Claiming that it would result in a $20 million loss for Twentieth Century Fox, he said, 'You've got to take the rough with the smooth.'

Talking about the film's rather vitriolic reception, Scott remarked during an interview in 2007, 'I think Russell did brilliantly in *A Good Year*. He and I loved that film and Fox loved it, and then they didn't know what to do and we got beaten up. Russell got beaten up mercilessly, which I thought was disgraceful because I genuinely thought we had done a good movie about a man in transition which is also quite funny. And what's really irritating and annoying is that I kept getting told later by actors, journalists, people outside of the industry, how much they enjoyed it. So anyway, fuck 'em. It was a good film.'

In another interview he said, 'We basically got fundamentally beaten up mercilessly by the British press and French press. At the end of the day, you can't give a shit. All you can do is actually be your own critic. That's key. Doing what we do, you have to be your own critic and judge and adjudicate as to what you do and how it turned out. How it turned out, I look at it and I'm very happy about it. Actually I was thrilled with this and the process was really great. Apart from that, it was great fun.'

The film will always hold a special memory for Russell, as his second son was conceived at the French chapel used as one of the film's locations. In fact the mayor of Bonnieux offered Tennyson Crowe honorary citizenship. He said, 'It would give us great pleasure if one day, during a trip to France, they stop by Bonnieux so we can make their baby an honorary citizen.'

CHAPTER TWENTY

CROWE SADDLES UP AGAIN

'We're doing the same job but coming at it from opposite directions and it's like a joust.'

– Ridley Scott

Next up for Russell would be *3:10 to Yuma* in 2007 – a remake of the 1957 Western, itself based on the 1953 short story by Elmore Leonard. It saw Russell team up with one of Hollywood's most respected young actors – Christian Bale.

The *Batman* star, no stranger himself to a fiery reputation, said he'd harboured some trepidation about working with Russell. 'We'd never met before and whenever people asked me what I was doing next and I said I was going to be working with Russell, they looked at me and said, "You're going to be in for a rough ride with him." [But] it was truly a pleasure.'

It's no surprise that the pair bonded, although Bale did have to put up with Russell's constant teasing about his superhero past. 'It never stopped and it continues still. I actually had to buy him his own special rubber suit.'

Bale also had a reputation for going to extreme lengths to get in the mind of his characters – witness his skeletal look in *The Machinist* – and even Russell would have to sit back and admire his dedication.

Bale's tendency to keep the accent was something that Russell was amazed at, knowing that it was something that he could never do. 'If I did that at home, my wife would just be like, "Forget about it, man. I ain't sleeping with Buffalo Bill."'

With Russell's ranch experiences, and having enjoyed his previous horse-riding films, it was a shoot he enjoyed immensely. 'Probably since I was about nine or 10 years old I've ridden horses quite regularly, and I have a cattle farm. I have my own horses and stuff, so for me that was just a pleasure. Being actually able to be on horseback for nine or 10 hours a day wasn't worrying me at all. You know, the more the better.'

And there was one particular scene he enjoyed – seeing director James Mangold struggling to cope with the environment that he was so used to. 'Working with the horses and the cattle weren't his favourite moments. He had a cracker of a time at one point where Jim thought he was going to be able to stampede cattle and they would take a left turn just because that's how he marked the path.

'I was trying to catch him. I said, "Jimmy, mate, it

don't work that way. You stampede those cattle they're gonna go up that hill, and we're gonna be hanging around here for two hours getting the cattle down from the hill." He goes, "No, but the path's marked clearly." "It's a fucking cow! It's not gonna go around the corner like that." He said, "OK, let's see what happens."

'We did see what happened. Bang! Bang! They stampeded and up the bloody mountain they went, and two hours later we're still twiddling our thumbs waiting for the cattle to come down from the top of the mountain.'

There was a different kind of trouble when a freak storm hit the set, blasting the crew with freezing temperatures. Visitors to the set would have been stunned to have been given hand-warmers in the normally hot surroundings, while truckloads of dirt were being driven in to cover the snowy conditions.

Russell formed a close bond with his horse during the shoot, and admitted it was tough to part company. 'Doing these sort of movies with animals, you get close because it's an intense working relationship – 10 or 12 hours a day for months – so it's hard to say goodbye. There are some you have a deeper connection with immediately and you can work on that over time. I've found over the years that the more gentle you are with a horse, the deeper that connection gets.'

The film was a hit with critics, with many calling it an improvement on the original. 'Here the quality of the acting, and the thought behind the film, make it seem like a vanguard of something new, even though it's a remake of a good movie 50 years old,' said Roger Ebert.

Russell would team up with Ridley again in *American Gangster*. Documenting the tale of a 1970s crime lord, a *New Yorker* magazine article titled *The Return of the Superfly* proved to be the inspiration for Russell's next project.

The story of how Frank Lucas masterminded an operation to distribute some of the strongest heroin to hit New York City through his ingenious plan of smuggling the ingredients directly from Vietnam in the coffins of dead US solders is a compelling, exciting and thrilling one. It was ripe for the big screen.

That's not to say that it didn't have problems getting there. If the first attempt to get the story made hadn't fallen through, you would have seen a completely different movie. It would have had Terry George on directing duties, with Don Cheadle and Joaquin Phoenix playing the Denzel Washington and Russell characters respectively.

The second attempt would have seen Washington reunite with his *Training Day* director, Antoine Fuqua, with Benicio Del Toro playing detective Richie Roberts. Spiralling costs, however, saw them ditch the film a second time, despite filming being only weeks away.

But Washington, who was still paid for his involvement in the movie despite it being axed because of his pay-or-play deal, hadn't give up hope on the project.

The film's producer, Brian Grazer, commissioned the

script as soon as he read the article. He said, 'I really love this story. It's haunted me from the first time I was told about it and I just couldn't give up on it. I knew that Denzel loved the role and I learned later on that he still had contact with Frank Lucas – that's how much he liked the role and understood it. So, once I got Ridley Scott to say yes to the movie, Denzel said he would do it again.'

Scott said about making the film: 'I've known Steve [Zallian – the film's writer] for a long time. We're friends and we worked together on *Hannibal* and he helped me out on *Black Hawk Down*. If Steve calls me and asks me to read something, I will, whether I'm going to work on it or not. If he just wants my opinion, that's fine.

'I first read it about three and a half years ago and I loved it – great characters, great time period, great feeling. Actually, I don't know whether I was getting offered it or not back then, but I couldn't do it anyway because I was about to start on *Kingdom of Heaven*. But then when I was doing *A Good Year* with Russell I heard it had problems and wasn't happening and I said to Russell, "Have you read it? What do you think? Let's make this work..." And the fact is he knows Brian and I know Brian, so we both called him.'

Russell had worked on two of Grazer's films – *A Beautiful Mind* and *Cinderella Man* – and at the same time as Grazer was trying to convince Scott to direct the picture, he sent the script to Russell in the hope he would star alongside Washington.

Russell was to play an honest if roguish and womanising New York detective called Richie Roberts.

Grazer said of the two lead characters, 'One guy was an extreme version of a gangster and the other guy was like the perfect cop, the personification of what America thought her police officers should be. Richie Roberts even turned down a $1 million take!

'He was an aberration at a time when there were so many corrupt cops. One guy, Lucas, has this great home life, a real family man, and the other, Roberts, wrecks his marriage because of his affairs. And these two huge characters are headed on a collision course.'

Talking about Washington's character, who took over a small crime organisation when his mentor died, Grazer added, 'But he just didn't take it over, he took it to a whole new level and flooded Harlem with heroin. Frank Lucas was an entrepreneur not much different from any kind of white-collar entrepreneur who does things that are corrupt and involves the lives of other people. He was kind of the flip side of the American Dream.'

Washington added, 'It wasn't a case of him walking around being the tough guy all the time. He laughs a lot, cries a lot, and he's not a bad guy – he's just had this violent and unbelievable past. It's like he said to me: "I was in a dirty business and there was only one way to do it. There wasn't any room for nice guys." It's not like there's your friendly neighbourhood heroin dealer.'

The film rested on the pair's shoulders, but it was a

burden they had no problem with. The pair had remained close friends after starring together in *Virtuosity* and were keen to team up again.

Russell said of the moment that sealed their friendship in 1995, 'About halfway through the shoot, Denzel came to my trailer one night with two cigars and a bottle of cognac. He knocked on the door and was like, "Shall we have a drink?" And I was like, "Cool, come on in."

'So we sat there and we were chatting for about half an hour, 40 minutes, and I always remembered something he said, and for me doing *American Gangster* is a partial payback for him. He said, "You know, I've never said this to any other actor, but man, I wish I was playing your role." So when I got the *Gangster* script, and I knew how much Denzel wanted to do it – I read it and the thing is, what's great about it is the character of Frank Lucas. On the page it was Frank and really there wasn't any other half at that time. There was nothing else going on. And that conversation, all those years ago, came to mind, because I'm reading it going, "Man, I wish I was playing Frank!" So the process of getting involved in this is really a form of repaying him, a certain loyalty from 12 years ago.'

As before on many of Russell's films, he and Scott set about 'beefing' up the character of Roberts, with both agreeing that it was somewhat underwritten and Russell conceding that the character 'needed a lot more work'.

'But you know what, we've done that before. We did it with *Gladiator* and to a lesser extent we did it with *A Good Year*.'

Scott could be happy that he had two leads who could both dominate films on their own with their presence and charisma and wouldn't be overshadowed by each other. And juggling two movie stars with movie-star baggage was doable, despite the many headaches caused by their constant moaning about the script. 'We just sat in a room on our own and went over it again and again. And you know, these two are very similar – they want to know things are happening the way they should. That's fine, I understand that.

'They are always complaining. And they get pretty passionate when they complain. They're always complaining about the writer. And I'm going, "Well, actually the writer is pretty fucking good..." This is not just Denzel, this is Russell as well. I mean, fucking hell! And I'm going, "I disagree. I think he's fantastic, that's why I'm here, right?"

'We're doing the same job but coming at it from opposite directions and it's like a joust. And I'm seeing it as part of my job to let them see it how it could be and they are saying, "Yes, but I need this." And so I will supply that as much as I can, help them as much as possible with that kind of discussion.'

He added, 'But now I've just learnt that's what they do and there's no taming the beast, believe me. You have to let them agonise. With the best it's part of the process – and we are talking about two of the best here.'

But, he conceded, 'It gets to a point of craziness where there are too many cooks in the kitchen. Somebody has got to be the chef and somebody has to say, "No, wash your hands, you don't chop onions that way."'

Talking about his character, Russell said, 'Well, I didn't know anything about Richie. He wasn't like a big feature in what we knew of Frank Lucas, so I wanted to know about him and who he was. The thing I found out was that he was a true patriot – he came out of school, had a look around and decided to become a Marine. He went into the Marine corps and whatever he discovered didn't really satisfy him so he went into the police force. And what he discovered there didn't satisfy him either, so he went to law school and became a prosecutor. And that didn't satisfy him either.

'Every one of these American institutions that he went into, in the country he absolutely believed in, was affected by some kind of benign corruption, so he ended up becoming a defence attorney because he could still be a patriot from that point of view. He could be an advocate for people without defence, stand up for people who required defence, and he could stand on the outside of the castle and chuck rocks. He could say: "I don't care if you're the president, it's my duty to ask what the fuck you're doing, mate." So he stuck to his guns, and he stayed an idealist and he's still a patriot. I really respect him for that.'

As research for playing Richie Roberts, Russell interviewed some of New York's toughest characters, but his meeting with them didn't go the way he expected. 'With the first couple I met, I couldn't work out why they were shaking. I thought they must've been dealing with some sort of extreme drug problem or something like that. But then one of the gangsters I was doing the interview with said about the other one, "No, don't worry. He's just fucking nervous. He's nervous because he's being interviewed by Maximus!"

'This is a guy who may well have been responsible for killing people, but a movie star is a movie star.'

The real life Lucas was an ever-present member during filming, Scott revealed to *Empire*. 'Frank was on set every day. And I found him to be quite straightforward. I'd ask him questions like, "Did anything intimidate you?" And nothing did. I mean, he's a guy who flew to Saigon where there's a war going on and does a deal which is going to run for the next five years.

'Then you infiltrate the US Army there, through your cousin, and you do a deal with a two-star general, you organise helicopter pilots to move the dope, and pilots of transporters who are bringing it back to America in the bottom of the coffins of dead GIs – all on a payola, a backhander of $5,000 here or $10,000 there. I said to Frank, "You must have been worried." He just shrugged and said, "What about?" He genuinely didn't know what I meant.'

Talking about his encounter with the real life Roberts, who would also visit the set but far less frequently, Scott revealed, 'I'd talk to Richie about the corruption. You know, "How bad was it?" And he'd say, "Don't make it look like everyone was on the take, because they weren't, but there was a lot going on." So I'd take that on board.'

One scene saw Russell's character attending the 1971 boxing match between Muhammad Ali and Smokin' Joe Frasier at Madison Square Garden. After their attempts to film at the same venue fell through, they plumped for the Long Island ice hockey Nassau Veterans Memorial Coliseum instead. 'We couldn't afford Madison Square Garden,' Ridley said. 'I didn't want to afford it. They wanted $350,000 for one evening and I said, "That's crazy!" The sequence is four minutes long, so bollocks. We went to the hockey stadium and it looks just like it.'

Josh Brolin, who played Detective Trupo, admitted he was so nervous about starring with Russell that he feared his subsequent acting performance and wardrobe malfunction was going to get him fired. 'I was a little plumper than I wanted to be. I justified it that the character's tough and he needs to be plumper. I came to the set, they put the wardrobe on me and it was tight. I just get through my nerves with Russell, and improvise a little bit. I grab a chair and when I sat down the ass of my pants ripped right open. Usually, that's a great icebreaker, but I did the worst acting I've ever done in my life. I was shaking, I was nervous.'

'I got back to my trailer, took off my pants, gave them to wardrobe and went to my trailer waiting to get fired. I finally got a knock on the door and Ridley says, "Josh, I don't know what you're doing, but you're bringing an incredible vulnerability to this role."'

However, Brolin would later complain about working with Russell. In 2009, he was talking about his *Milk* co-star Sean Penn when he said, 'Quite the actor, that Sean Penn. He's not an asshole like Russell Crowe.' Although, he did later explain, 'It was the ambience of the room. I love him. I think he's amazing. I was bummed out when I saw that. He's a friend.'

Russell's detective team in the film seemed to enjoy his company – particularly on their last day of filming, which saw them rammed into Russell's cluttered trailer, which was piled high with scripts, family mementos and gym equipment, to enjoying a drink.

'They were fucking great, mate. And that bonding was very, very important, because on screen we had to look like we knew each other inside out, look like we're comfortable with one another. Richie Roberts and the guys on the investigation were very close and we needed to be exactly the same way.'

There was also the problem of a $60 million lawsuit being filed by a group of retired Drug Enforcement Agents, who objected to the portrayal of DEA agents in the film. A judge threw out the case, however, with Universal Pictures saying that they were delighted that the matter had been brought to 'a swift and decisive close'.

New Yorker magazine was also angered that the film described the story as an original screenplay rather than an adapted one. Universal claimed *The Return of Superfly* magazine article was 'used as a research material' only, and that many of the characters seen in the film were not in the article.

Better news came from the box office, with the film nearly taking $50 million in the US alone on the opening weekend. Universal distribution president Nikki Rocco said, 'It's a great movie, and the timing was perfect to jump-start the business. The picture was well done and well marketed, and it was placed in the market at a time when its adult audience could embrace it.'

The film was generally well received by critics. Roger Ebert called it 'an engrossing story' and the *Wall Street Journal* a 'great big gangster film, and a good one', although The *Baltimore Sun* dismissed it as a 'Scorcese, Coppola or De Palma cover version'.

Scott was pleased with thc film, saying, 'It's nice to see a film, isn't it? It's a film. A proper film with no tricks. There's no CGI. Nothing.'

CHAPTER TWENTY-ONE

BODY OF LIES

'The great actors are never easy.'

– Ridley Scott

'Information is the bottom line and the subtext of that could be that you cannot trust anyone, not even your best friend. Turn your back for a second and you will be used. And if you are running an organisation that is important to national security, without the attitude you will be weaker and vulnerable. That's the job,' surmised Scott about his and Russell's next venture, *Body of Lies* (2008).

It was based on a book by novelist and *Washington Post* columnist David Ignatius, who had covered stories in the Middle East. Scott was fascinated by the source material. 'The characters and David Ignatius's view I think is mostly the truth. If you're a *Washington Post* journalist for 30 years, foreign correspondent, he is fluent in Arabic... his passion, he's obviously a romantic, his passion is the Middle East. When you read his book you get a full sense that you're reading the truth. All he's done is change the names.'

Ignatius said, 'This really began from work I did with Ridley on an earlier project. In the course of that we got to know each other so when I finished the first draft of *Body of Lies* I let Ridley know about it.

'When I finished the book I had a different title. It was called *Penetration* because it told what agents do, which is penetrate their adversary. Penetration these days for most folks sounds like an X-rated movie. That seemed to be the opinion of most folk, but Ridley liked it.'

Five weeks before shooting began, Scott told MTV, 'It's based on David Ignatius' book, which originally was called *Penetration*, and then it was called *Body of Lies*. So we're still wrestling with the title. There's another interesting title called *Chatter*.

'So send in which one you like,' he joked, suggesting an online poll. 'It's between *Chatter*, *Penetration* or *Body of Lies*. It's not about sex; it's about politics in the Middle East, and it's really good.' They ended up keeping the *Body of Lies* title.

Despite being one of the most influential and successful directors in Hollywood, Scott found it difficult to get the movie made. 'It always is, but you can't really think about it. I read the manuscript 19 months ago, went, "Wow", negotiated, bought it, found a writer, negotiate, got him writing. That was slow, wasn't too happy. That took a few months. I'd delivered *American Gangster* and

I'm staring at this material which then needs a lot of work on it. In that time, the world's constantly changing. All you can do is make sure that you deliver what you feel is the best you can do.

'In Hollywood there's some of the smartest and toughest motherfuckers you're ever likely to meet. A really bad combination. Also, the most uneasy thing is where they recognise passion as a weakness. If they know you want to do something, you're gonna pay for that. You have to hide the fact that you're really desperate to do it.'

The film's writer, William Monahan, said, 'David Ignatius's book was a very complicated thriller. My job was to capture the essence of the book, while compressing it as a film. The usual problem on doing movies from books is that the ideal way is fourteen Tuesday nights but we have to make it a two-hour movie. And in here the compression was arduous.

'I had to go away for a week to a house on the East Coast to get away from everybody and cut basically 30 pages from the script that I didn't want to lose. Everything was good. I said to David that you could do another movie from the book.'

The book certainly focused more on the nitty-gritty work of being a CIA operative, with Russell's Hoffman character pushed more into the background. Hoffman is CIA operative Roger Ferris's (played by DiCaprio) control at CIA headquarters in Langley. Ignatius said, 'I think this larger story of the CIA abroad and its efforts to recruit people, is a process of seduction and abandonment, both of the people that they work with and sometimes its own employees. It's a theme that's fascinated me in all my books. We're living through a period right now where we're seeing how horrific intelligence operations can be. I think one of strengths of the movie is that it does transcend the here and now and tells a story that could be told about the agency at any point in its history or its future. It's a basic dynamic that surrounds their work.'

Getting Russell wasn't as easy as Scott would have liked, either. 'I called him up and said do you want to do this?

'He said, "I want the lead part," I said, "You can't, Leo's got that." He said, "He's got the best part."

'I said, "Not necessarily – think of your part as a character study." That always appeals to him. I said, "He can be stocky, have bad knees from football, looks after the kids, is bullied by the wife, but is master of the universe. He probably has a box at the CIA where he doesn't have to answer to anyone, can do what the fuck he wants and he's a bastard, but he actually drives the kids to school."

He said, "OK, I'll do it."''

Russell's version of events differed somewhat. 'The first thing that I got was a phone call from Ridley saying, "How'd you like to put on a large amount of weight?"

And that always appeals to me, so that was a sell right there. He said that he wanted Hoffman to feel like an ex-football player with bad knees who still had some grace about him. Everything else comes from the book and the way the character talks.'

Talking about the film, Russell said in the production notes, 'Obviously, it's a movie and is not meant to be taken as fact, but it was important to me to give people an idea of what it really takes, in terms of deception, to operate an organisation like the CIA, especially in a place where there's a definite culture clash. You have to stand back a long way to see where that river runs.

'At Hoffman's level, it's not a matter of being a chess player. It's about being able to see seven different chessboards situated on seven different planes, and manipulating all those multiples of seven simultaneously.'

Talking on the film's DVD commentary, Scott revealed, 'Russell loves to take on completely different personas and also take on physical differences. You saw it when he did *The Insider*. That's part of his art. He thinks it's important – the physical appearance, the hair, the accent. That's why I like working with him; he's 100 per cent all out.

'I was up for Hoffman being in no offices. We never even had an office set for Hoffman, so his set was his kitchen, his back garden, his kid's school, his garden, a restaurant. Because of that he's always eating.'

Ignatius recalled, 'The first time I talked to Russell he

asked me, "Where's Hoffman from?" And I said, "I don't know." I said, "Maybe he's from Massachusetts. I kind of can imagine Worcester or some working-class town in Massachusetts," and Russell said, "No, he's not. He's from Arkansas."

'And he had decided that that was where this character was from and that's how this character was going to talk. They obviously re-imagined the characters in a hundred different ways, and that's now who these people are. I'll never be able to read the book and read about Hoffman and not think about Russell, and the same thing with Ferris and Leo.'

For Russell it meant teaming up again with his *The Quick and the Dead* co-star Leonardo DiCaprio. The pair had become close friends while working on the film. 'You had Gene Hackman and Sharon Stone and these actors who had been in the business for 30 years. We had only done a couple of small movies, and we weren't part of that superstar club. So we forged a friendship and started our own club', Russell said.

'Working with him is a little like hopping on a train' said DiCaprio. 'You just have to have faith and make that leap. But once you're on, you realise how focused he really is.'

Russell, meanwhile, had harboured some concerns about his pal after seeing him propelled to superstardom in *Titanic*. 'I was a little worried about him after *Titanic*. The massive success of something like that, it's not always a positive, particularly when you're that young. Suddenly you find yourself on lunchboxes and bedroom slippers. That can have a deteriorating effect on the inside.'

This time most of their scenes were of them talking on phones, with Russell saying, 'It's the same as if you're doing a CGI film and you're supposed to be floating in a flock of black ravens. In fact, most of the time when you're on a film set, what you see in the audience has nothing to do with the experience of the actor.

'So you've always got to be shutting off things that are going to affect your focus and all that sort of stuff. So it's the same sort of thing where you just zero in on the phone call. Some guys try to attempt to do that thing of having both people on the phone at the same time which is just utterly a waste of time. It's better that you just do the groove by yourself.

'And then if you shot it first, the next person gets to hear where you were and they will fold into that, or if you're doing it second, it's the same thing. You listen to what they said and then you have a think about it.'

Scott, having worked with the vocal team of Russell and Washington, was again pairing his regular collaborator with a heavyweight A-Lister – and again he was faced with a pairing that didn't keep quiet if they aren't happy with the script. 'Both actors get into it in a very big way. They're in it from the word go. They're in it from the book, through to "Who's the writer?" through to constant readjustments of the script. This happens right up to the first week of principal photography.'

'So they're encouraged – well, not Russell and Leo, they're not going to be shy in coming forward, believe me! – but I mean, if I've got someone coming in new, like Mark Strong – I hadn't worked with him before and I really enjoyed that experience – so I liked to include him in the process. Everything, right down to how he looks. What do you think, what do you think, what do you think?'

It's a process that Scott likes. He doesn't do a lot of rehearsals, so he likes every actor to do their homework – forming and creating their characters before they appear in front of the camera.

Russell said of filming with Scott, 'People make the assumption that we agree on everything. That's ridiculous. On any subject we have an instinctive disagreement about 70 per cent of the time. But over time we've perfected the art of the wordless argument, and we enjoy the process of problem-solving.

'The thing about me and Ridley is I really listen to him, which I think scares him sometimes. But he appreciates it because he'll say something to me early on and then get really involved in all of the other details. But he knows I'll keep the integrity of his original concepts alive as we go through the arc of the story.'

Talking about the closeness of their relationship, DiCaprio – or 'the new guy' as called himself – remarked,

'They have such a shorthand together, they know how to solve problems immediately. I embrace that kind of energy. It's really rewarding and exhilarating to work with these type of people. Once you've rehearsed the scene and established the arc of what the outcome should be, Ridley gets all the cameras up and it's go time. And Russell is intensely real and very present.

'I just think he is one of the great actors of our time, so it was great to go at him again. We had some powerfully dynamic, combative scenes together in this film. You relish these moments when you have another actor sitting across from you that can match everything you do and give more back. It's an adrenaline rush.'

Praising Russell's performance, producer Donald De Line said, 'Russell brings a lot of levity and humour to Hoffman, which I didn't expect. Hoffman is a morally questionable character, and you're not always sure how you feel about him. But he's so straightforward about who he is and what he believes, it's kind of refreshing. You almost can't begrudge him for it.'

Russell had gained weight for the part – something which amused DiCaprio, who admitted that he 'couldn't stop' laughing at his pal's newfound bulk. Russell's yo-yo weight gain and loss depending on the part was taking its toll, and after *Body of Lies* he was forced to take a health check after an embarrassing incident. 'At one point I worried about it from a health point of view because I had my cholesterol checked. It had reached dangerous territory. I was surprised that my body was taking all of it so seriously. I was enjoying myself, because I was eating and drinking what I liked, but my body was objecting. The most frightening thing was having to rock back and forwards to get out of a car. Instead of stepping out, I had to tip myself out.'

Scott wanted to film in Dubai, but the film's searing political theme was too controversial for the federation's National Media Council, who refused to give permission. The CEO of Filmworks, Tim Smyth, whose Dubai-based company were hired by Warner Bros to set up shooting there, said, 'After receiving approval, it was later rejected, as Dubai does not want to do any scripts that are of a political nature.

'It's unfortunate and limits the options of films to come to Dubai to help develop the industry, as to date 85 per cent of all films we have been approached about have some form of political nature.

Talking about shooting on location, Scott said, 'This is the fourth time I've filmed in North Africa, so I'm something of an expert. I knew what I could do with the locations.'

The film's Middle East Technical Advisor and Consultant, Sam Sako, said, 'Mr Scott has a good background here. He has shot four films in Morocco, so I call him Scott of Arabia. He has been in this country for such a long time he should buy a villa and just shoot films here. Why not?'

One of the more intense scenes saw Leonardo DiCaprio's character being tortured. Scott recalls of shooting that scene: 'In *Alien* the studio said, "Gee you're gross!" and I said, "Hang on, I'm paid to be gross!" because that was a horror movie. In this instance it's tricky because now we're dealing with a horrible reality. So I have to imagine what it would really be like... But also we've got good text, we've got good words, and we've got great actors. So in the end, it's theatre.'

DiCaprio added, 'We knew that there was this pivotal end moment in the movie where I'm in the hands of the enemy. This was something I think I knew way back when Bill Monahan first gave me the script and told me about this project, and told me about Ridley and about the whole relationship. We talked about that scene. This was the scene that needed to be the pivotal moment in the film, that unless that worked and was believable and had the guts to it and the intensity to it and the weight, the film wouldn't work almost.

'It was something we talked about at great length and analysed in every possible direction. What would a CIA agent trying to do his best in this world finally say if he's in that situation? What are the words that would come out of his mouth? What kind of tactics would he use to try to get out of the situation? What is he thinking about? Is he thinking about his own survival, the betterment of his country, what secrets does he release?

'It was one of the more complimented scenes for the

movie and one of the most intense in the sense that we knew we had to knock it out of the park. I actually got sick after the scene for three days because there was just so much intensity put into that.'

Taking only $13 million in its first week in the US, the film seemed to split the critics. The main consensus was that despite its gritty look and topical subject matter, it resorted to the clichés of the spy thriller of old. However, it wouldn't be too far fetched to assume that maybe the world didn't need this kind of film at a time when the news was saturated with similar content.

Not that that was a surprise to the people involved making the film. Russell said before filming, 'It's machinations and creations of the American government, in terms of its foreign policy. I don't think it's so responsive to what's happening now – because what's happening now is actually the fruit of seeds planted two or three decades ago, if not more. But I think it's timely to do a movie like that... it's important, and Ridley is up for [portraying] the true negatives of this web of intrigue that's been created.'

'I don't think it will be very popular. But that's never been part of my project choice process.'

CHAPTER TWENTY-TWO

READ ALL ABOUT IT

'I've been praised, flayed and betrayed, and those experiences obviously are going to colour the way I think.'

– Russell Crowe

The crime drama *Tenderness* was released in 2008. It's an unremarkable thriller directed by a filmmaker (John Polson) who made the unremarkable *Swimfan* and *Hide and Seek*. Not that's it's a terribly bad movie, but it's so run-of-the-mill it's hard to see what appealed to Russell. Following that, however, would be *State of Play*.

Harking back to the political conspiracy thrillers of the 1970s, *State of Play* – based on the highly praised 2003 BBC mini-series – is rammed with ice-cool assassins, shadowy figures lurking in parking lots and journalists intent on discovering the truth.

When talking about bringing the TV series to the big screen, producer Andrew Hauptman said, 'The original series was such a rare find in source material. It was a riveting series that grabbed you and didn't let go; it resonated with me in so many ways. I always thought that by moving the setting to Washington DC, its scope could be even more powerful and combustible, but just as intelligent.

'The opportunity to get inside the world of the newsroom and feel the drama associated with running a paper, chasing a story and the pursuit of the truth and all of its implications brought a lot of relevance to the story. What made the mini-series work so well was that on the surface it was about the dance between politics and journalism – the state of contemporary news media, corporate espionage and conspiracy. But then you realise it was also about individuals and their choices and was deeply personal. It tackled issues of conflict and compromise, loyalty and love, and power and career aspirations. That made it incredibly intriguing.'

Director Kevin Macdonald tried to shy away from the series as much possible. For one thing, cramming six hours into two was always going to be a challenge and secondly, the BBC mini-series was an intricate, tightly woven beast and a cheap imitation would be met with indifference at best. Also Paul Abbott, who created the mini-series, was reluctant to sell the film rights.

Macdonald's slant then was to focus on the journalism angle more than the politics. What interested him in particular was the rapidly escalating tension between newspapers and online journalists.

'[I] deliberately left it behind. What we did was take some of the basic elements that were in the story then reinvent the rest of it and make it into its own thing. It can only live and breathe if it feels original, different,' he told *Digital Spy*. 'I wanted to make a film about the state of journalism and what's going on with newspapers. There's a real crisis, newspapers are under threat of closing down. That seemed like a really important topic to get to grips with.'

Macdonald made the comments during the London premiere of the film, with Russell adding that it was the 'rise of new media against traditional media' that interested him.

But it wasn't Russell who was supposed to play Cal McAffrey, the hard-nosed reporter who finds his loyalty to his former college roommate – now a rising congressman – under threat when he becomes part of the story that McAffrey is working on. Brad Pitt had long been attached to the project through his production company Plan B Entertainment.

Pitt, who quit his journalism major in the 1980s to pursue acting, took a big interest in the project after seeing the mini-series and liking Macdonald's previous movie, *The Last King of Scotland*. Despite his going to the *Washington Post* to research the part, the working relationship fell apart over the script. Pitt wanted to steer the film closer to the original draft by Matthew Michael Carnahan, while Macdonald wanted more rewrites.

The impending writers strike at the end of 2007 meant that the studio were keen to press on with the movie, fearing any delays would put the film under threat. Pitt, on the other hand, was keen to halt the film's production until they had a script he was happy with. 'I had definite beliefs of what [the film] should be, and the director had his definite beliefs [and] we got up against this writers' strike where we couldn't fuse the two,' Pitt said later.

Defending Pitt's decision to leave the project, Russell told *The Daily Record*, 'He's a very busy fella with a whole bunch of things on his plate. I know what it's like to develop something to the nth degree but not to want to step over and do it.'

Pitt's exit meant that the film was two weeks away from beginning filming without one the main characters cast. The director decided to head to Australia to try and get Russell's interest. Despite not have having seen the BBC mini-series, Russell was aware of how highly regarded the show was and he was also keen to work with Edward Norton, the original choice to play congressman Stephen Collins.

However, to add to the complications, Ed Norton decided to leave the project following Pitt's decision to depart. Ben Affleck took on the part instead, a casting decision that Russell agreed with. Despite having been keen to lock horns with Norton, he was also excited about working with Affleck.

Among those rounding out the cast were Rachel

McAdams as Della, the blogger who teams up with McAffrey, Dame Helen Mirren as the newspaper editor, and Jason Bateman as the Washington fixer.

After finishing *Body of Lies*, Russell had been keen to take a short break from working to spend time with his family before embarking on Ridley Scott's *Robin Hood*. So when he was asked to work on *State of Play* because of his close relationship with Universal studios, he was secretly hoping that he wouldn't be impressed enough to work on it. However, after watching *The Last King of Scotland* (Macdonald's feature film debut) and with the script passing his goose-bump test, he knew he had to be involved.

'I had never seen the mini-series so it came to me as a fresh piece and I felt I could make my own comment on it,' Russell explained. 'But I had not been predisposed to do this role, in any way, shape or form. I'd just come back from Morocco and various parts of Europe. I was back in Australia, the sun was shining, it was summer time and I really didn't want to have any conversations about work. But I got a call from Universal, with whom I have a very strong relationship.

'The sum total of our work together has been *Gladiator*, *A Beautiful Mind*, *Cinderella Man*, *American Gangster* and now this. They're not just work relationships, they're friendships. They explained to me that they are in a deep situation, in a bit of trouble with it, and would I please look at this script?'

He added, 'The first thing I did was look at Kevin's work, hoping I could easily dismiss it. But you can't easily dismiss *Touching the Void*, and you can't easily dismiss *The Last King of Scotland*. They're both great pieces. So that was my first bothersome moment. Then I read the script.

'I've had a rule since I was a kid that if I have a physical reaction to a script, if I get goose bumps, if a tear comes to my eye, that's a project that I have to do. That's being respectful of the gods of film. That's the reason I got into the job in the first place, because I want to tell the stories that emotionally affect me. So, it became, "There goes my summer holiday."'

Mirren said of Russell's casting, 'Obviously I wanted the film to happen, that's the most important thing. When Brad fell out it became a question mark, and luckily Russell came and saved us all.'

To prepare for the role, Russell made a conscious decision not to watch the 2003 mini-series. 'I was aware of *State of Play* but haven't seen it. I haven't and I'm not going to see it. It's six hours of finely crafted BBC television and it's not something you can compare, really. It would probably just make me angry if I watched it, because no doubt it's full of really lovely details and lots of cross-connections with characters and stuff. Where possible we've done that here, but essentially it's a different form and there's a big difference between two hours and six hours. A huge difference.'

With Macdonald hiring a journalist for the shoot – the editor of *The Washington Post*'s metro section, RB Brenner, Russell found a valuable source of information for the part. 'We talked about tactics when you go out on a story – how do you interview someone who doesn't want to give out information? – even down to little details like, if you want to knock on someone's door, how do you do it?' said Brenner.

Russell duly acknowledged that Brenner had 'been great because he's been able to explain things directly from the perspective of a newspaper.'

Macdonald could now see that Pitt's decision to leave the project was something of a blessing. 'In a way, I was lucky it didn't work out with Brad,' he said. 'The relationship between the journalist and the politician was meant to be between somebody who feels inferior – who's a bit of a schlump, who can't get a girlfriend – and somebody he's looking up to and admires – his polished politician friend. That is not the dynamic of Brad Pitt. He's not looking up to anyone thinking "Oh, I wish I could have your girlfriend."'

With Russell, it was different. Talking in the film's *Making of* documentary, Macdonald said, 'Russell came in and took the character by the scruff of the neck. The thing is with Russell, rather than do that in the superficial Hollywood way – Russell just took that and said, "OK, I'm going to be eating chilli dogs, I'm going to have the messiest apartment on earth, I'm going to be the nightmare you never want your daughter to go out with," and he created that. That's why he's a great actor. It's all about servicing the character, and not many movie stars are like that.'

The film's costume designer, Jacqueline West, said, 'The one great note that I got was that they never want to overdress – they always want the person they're interviewing to be at an advantage. Russell was so game for that. He loved the really gritty pictures of reporters that I showed him.'

Talking about his look for the film, Russell said, 'I had a much longer ponytail but Kevin didn't want that, even though I know many journalists and have met many who wear their hair in a long strand of ponytail. But the ill-shaped coats, the man bag, the ink stains on the shirt, these are all things that I brought to it, and all things that I've seen.'

Despite the fast turnaround of casting and with shooting rapidly approaching, the cast were determined to do as much research as possible. McAdams shadowed journalists at The *Washington Post*. 'They took us all over,' she said, 'and I met people who worked on line. I met young people and the people who have been doing it forever. There is a difference, there's a real shift. It's interesting.'

Macdonald must have been secretly delighted to see his two lead characters engage in the same combative manner that they inhabited in their characters. It all revolved around the scene when McAdams and Russell began disagreeing about their characters' motives when they debate whether they should hand over newly acquired photographs to the police.

'We got along really well,' McAdams told Collider.com. 'We really hit it off, so it developed naturally. We had a bit of a disagreement on our first meeting, which was true to our characters, so it was kind of perfect. We both had opposing viewpoints and were very stubborn and wouldn't relent. I can't remember who said what, but we were having an argument about something we were going to have an argument about. So we fell into it quite naturally and we became friends and I really enjoyed working with him. So it just happened that way.'

Macdonald was so impressed with the passion and intensity from the pair fighting their corner that he demanded the exchange be put in the script. Their stubborn streak was a boost for him, particularly in McAdams' case, seeing as it was proof that she wouldn't be overwhelmed by her more experienced co-stars.

McAdams did concede, however, that she was a little nervous to begin with. 'My first meeting was with both Russell and Helen at the same time. I admit I was a little shaky, a little nervous and my hands were even shaking when I shook Russell's hand. But it was great, they were all really supportive and I was really excited to be there.'

Talking about the pair's relationship on screen, Russell

remarked, 'Cal is sort of the dinosaur of the profession, while Della is the new kid on the block, or the new kid on the blog. She comes from a contemporary version of news gathering, where in a way it's more honest. You know, I have a little piece of information and I'm going to try to extrapolate that into something much larger if I just simply ask as many questions about it, and ask it myself.

'I think in a way that level of honesty of approaching a story offends Cal because he has spent the last 20 years or more being a reporter and gathering the information in a "credible" way, and not crossing certain boundaries, and being pretty sure of what he is writing before he writes it. But Della comes along with this fresh and contemporary attitude, and sort of shows up the older reporter as not as businesslike as he would pretend he is.'

Macdonald is the latest in a long list of directors who have gone on record about the intensity of working with an actor like Russell – someone who demands an input and is put off when it's not at the very least considered. 'Russell is highly opinionated,' he said. 'He is very smart, and he has his own ideas a lot of the time about how his character should be. Sometimes that would be great.

'It's collaboration with Russell. He has ideas about how he's going to do it, and it's hard sometimes to get him off that. He can be tough.'

Speaking at the premiere of the movie, Macdonald said more about his experiences working with Russell.

'There's a difference between an actor and a movie star. Russell manages to be both, but he's an actor first and foremost and he puts the character first.

'As a director, working with someone who's been the same in every movie, you'd have to mould the film around them, which is not what an actor should do. I think Russell enjoyed it but had a very complex relationship with the media and with journalists. He made that clear from the beginning – that he had some trepidation, because he wasn't sure he could play a heroic character as a journalist.

'And I think what we realised was that he didn't have to play a hero: the point of this character is that he is highly flawed. And like any journalist he makes mistakes, he has his biases, but in the long run he makes the right decisions, by his sense of the importance of his job and the integrity of what he's doing.'

Despite Russell's uncertainty about journalists, Brenner was impressed by his willingness and intuitiveness when playing a reporter. 'During his first tour of the newsroom set, he appeared jet-lagged and didn't ask many questions. A few days later, on camera, he ad-libbed a perfect line aimed at McAdams's character: "I've been here 15 years; I've got a 16-year-old computer. She's been here 15 minutes and she's got enough gear to launch a (expletive) satellite." He had noticed that the *Globe*'s online staff enjoyed snazzy new technology while the print reporters typed on clunky old equipment.

Somehow, without a hint from me, he picked up on a gripe you would hear in any print newsroom.

'In another scene, his character had to take notes. I sat by the video monitors, ready to correct him. His instincts took over. Every time a real reporter would have jotted a quote, he did. When nothing newsworthy was said, he listened.'

Brenner's involvement in the film was a great source of relief for Macdonald, as he learned that some of the journalism practices in the BBC drama wouldn't translate in America. As Brenner explained, '[The BBC series] portrays a Fleet Street world of newspapering that, though rollicking fun, is an ethical nightmare by American standards. Its ace reporter pays sources for information – an absolute no-no in the United States, surreptitiously videotapes a source in a hotel room – a firing offence and a felony in several states – and generally behaves like a walking conflict of interest.'

There were times, though, when Brenner's objections to the script were overruled. 'On the macro level, my crusade for authenticity bumped into unyielding walls at times. When I repeatedly objected to the illicit-videotaping scene, Macdonald politely made clear that in the end, plot rules. He was trying to tell a dramatic story, a political whodunit, and didn't want the audience bogged down in a journalism ethics lesson.

'I kept arguing that if he aspired to elevate the film above mere thriller, then accurately portraying my profession's code of conduct should matter more,' he added. 'The best I could manage was a hollow concession: McAdams's character objects to the sleazy behaviour and is overruled.'

However, Brenner's insistence on avoiding the impression that a 'reputable Washington reporter would ever consider paying for information' eventually paid off. Despite the script repeatedly calling for the journalists being asked to pay for a story, Russell's reporter 'never pays a dime'.

Not surprisingly, Russell didn't mince words on the film's overriding theme of the death of newspapers. 'There is a crisis in serious journalism and it's been created by journalists. We've been trivialising news for at least a couple of decades. The desire for new information, which we could use in a very healthy way, has been replaced by supplying trivia.

'I've sat in front of journalists for 30 years, so I have a lot of observational material to call on. I've been praised, flayed and betrayed, and those experiences obviously are going to colour the way I think. But it doesn't stop me from having a core belief that journalism is a noble profession.'

In an interview with the *Aberdeen Press and Journal*, he added, 'If you trivialise the news decade after decade, and if you turn news into entertainment, if you corrupt how people get information, if you have a cynical view where you can take a bit of fluff that's not true and you know it's not true, but you can bang it out to make something that fits nicely on page five next to the ad for women's lingerie – if you start thinking like that, then sooner or later people are going to distrust what those sources all are. We've built a generation that don't know how to discern bull from truth.'

Affleck, however, admitted he'd undergone a turnaround of opinion on journalists after starring in the film. In an interview with MTV, he stated: 'I definitely have a more full understanding of the pressures journalists face. My previous conversations with journalists were all one-sided. Even though I wasn't playing a journalist, the story is about empathising with a guy who is a journalist.

'[I now realise] that journalists are ambitious and competing with each other inside institutions, and that the institutions themselves have to compete with one another to stay afloat. I never understood those dynamics very well, so I've gained an appreciation for that, and it changed the way I saw things.'

Mirren, who played the newspaper's tough-as-nails editor, also spoke of her research. 'They kindly allowed us to sit in on what they call their "4 o'clock meeting", which is when they start shaping up the next day's newspaper. The head of each department pitches his or her own stories to try to get it on the front page. The feeling in that room was great. You felt you were in a room with very smart people, but they were also very tough with each other. No politeness, just very straightforward, very on the nose. You've got to have nerves of steel in that environment.'

State of Play received generally positive reviews, with many grateful for mainstream entertainment that catered to an adult audience. Indeed, one of the film's writers – Tony Gilroy – seems to have become a byword for popcorn entertainment for grown-ups thanks to his screenwriting work on the Jason Bourne series and the corporate thriller *Michael Clayton* (which he also directed).

Not everyone was impressed, however. The *A.C. Club* wrote: 'It's naïve about the way news-gathering and reporting works in the new media world; at one point, a major scoop is held so subscribers can absorb it with ink-stains on their fingers. Fat chance.'

It may not have enjoyed the best box office opening in the US, but in the UK it stormed to number one, knocking the CGI hit *Monsters vs Aliens* off the top spot.

CHAPTER TWENTY-THREE

RUSSELL AND THE MEDIA

'Russell doesn't necessarily see the noble side of my profession.'

– Journalist RB Brenner

During shooting of *The Insider*, which saw Russell made up to appear much older, he began to resemble his dad. One unwelcome byproduct of this was that his father had to experience what his son goes through on a regular basis. 'Dad was at the premiere in Los Angeles and he was being chased by photographers. And my dad is just a bloke, you know? And after the fourth one came running up taking his picture, he turned round and said, "Look, fuck off! I'm not him!"'

At first glance Russell and journalism have an uneasy relationship – he the no-nonsense Australian tough guy, they the sensation-seeking media desperate to rake up any dirt they can on him. But Russell, like most major movie stars, knows that the press are vital to anyone's dreams of conquering Hollywood. Film actors who don't buy into the Hollywood hype and all its baggage and still come out the other side as A-listers are few and far between. While Russell is arguably one of those success stories, he has also attempted to court the media in the past.

Journalist Jack Marx famously told all about his encounter with Russell Crowe. It started when the *Sunday Morning Herald* journalist received a phone call from the actor, asking to meet up for dinner. What happened afterwards would be a cautionary tale about journalists getting too close to their subject.

During the meeting, Marx was bombarded with questions about his personal life, with his meal left untouched because his mouth was busy answering questions about every aspect of his life. The last question, enquiring was how much he was paid, left Marx tantalised about the possibilities open to him. Thinking that the meeting could lead to a job with Russell – why else the money question, he reasoned? – he was nonetheless delighted when he was asked to attend a rugby game with the actor.

After several other phone calls leading to a meeting at his office, Marx was finally told the reason for the courting. Russell wanted someone to be a 'champion' for him in the media, particularly for his music career, for which he felt he was being unfairly criticised.

After agreeing to be such a champion, although he would wonder if he was making the right decision when making his Faustian pact, Marx was later asked to write an article about Russell by the film company behind his then new film, *Cinderella Man*. Marx claims that Russell revealed that the music mission was 'nothing more than a test'. His 'Machiavellian' plan was to make Marx his publicist. All that Russell needed was a positive article about him for the film.

Marx wrote in the *Sydney Morning Herald* article, 'There was a journalist in London... who had written many stories on [Russell], and as a consequence had enjoyed drinking with Russell in 22 cities of the world. This journalist had resisted all pressure to write bad Russell stories, and was thus much loved and rewarded. "So you see, Jack," he wrote, "not all journalists are cunts." He added that if I wanted to do the story, then, he was "cool with it".'

Marx wrote the piece, smoothing over some of the facts for a sympathetic portrayal of Russell rather than a gushing one. Nonetheless, Marx claimed that his piece was considered 'low and shitty' by Russell.

Marx's *Herald* article, which recounted his meetings with Russell in greater detail, painted the actor as a manipulative individual who had promised certain journalists the world if they posted positive articles about him.

Talking about his article further in *The Telegraph* in 2006, Marx said, 'Russell was clearly grooming me. Perhaps he never intended to make me his publicist –

that was just a carrot to dangle. But then he had no need to go to the lengths he did just to get a good interview. I did feel a bit dirty when I was sitting eating supper with him on his farm. A little voice in my head was warning me that this was not real friendship, but I ignored it. I was in denial that he saw this as just a showbiz transaction.'

Ironically, Russell had hit back at the idea that he uses the media in the first article that Marx had written about him. In it, Russell said, 'I think it is kind of ridiculous to imply I'm in cahoots or in bed with the media. A preposterous notion – a cynical reframing, more than likely, sourced from the same voices who, two years ago, were trumpeting my distance or aloofness as the problem.'

Another journalist, Martyn Palmer, who struck up a genuine friendship with the actor, had this to say about his friendship with Russell. 'He was 25 and at the start of his Australian film career and I'd been sent to interview him.

'We became unlikely friends. For reasons which neither of us has ever really analysed, we just got along. When he was in the UK, he'd camp at my place. When I was in Australia, I'd stay in the spare room, on a mattress, with a piano he was renovating and various guitars.'

He went on to say, 'He became, and remains, a kind of godfather figure to my two lads. He sends them presents, messages and pieces of priceless film memorabilia from all over the world. Once, on the set of *Gladiator*, a muddy Surrey wood doubling as a German forest in the days of ancient Rome, he plonked them both on the director and producer's chairs so that they could get the best view of him fighting the hordes.

'When the fame, the really big-time stuff, began to happen, he shared it like a bag of sweeties. In Cannes where *L.A. Confidential* was premiered in 1997, he dragged me – the journalist, aka the enemy – along to parties on private yachts. He organised a meeting between me and the writer James Ellroy because he knew I was a huge fan. Over the years, he's been more generous and fun to know in ways he probably wouldn't even like me to share with you. He once, for example, chartered a helicopter so that he could see my daughter on her twelfth birthday. The stories are endless.'

Another friend, the Australian musician Ray Di Pietro, said, 'There are people here he's known for a few years. Then he always meets new friends everywhere. It's not necessarily what you do, it's you. If he thinks you're a good, stand-up person, he wants you around. He's a good man.'

He's a guy that makes sure the cast and crew of his film from the stars up to the runners down each get a fleece top. 'It's a good way of making everyone part of a team, a good way of bonding. It's a small thing but I do like it.'

One of his best friends, the actor Simon Westaway said, 'Above everything, Russell understands the value of friendship. He's not motivated by money or power and when he acts, he's putting on a jacket. What he needs from me is loyalty and that's what he gives back.'

In one rant about the media, Russell accused them of exaggerating his reputation. 'There is a lot of just intentional misinformation as well. I've never had a fight with a photographer, for example, but you can find hundreds of articles on the net which will list me fighting with paparazzi, something I do apparently on a regular basis. But that's just not true. I just don't bother letting it bug me any more, and because it doesn't bug me, in this odd way, it happens less.'

In another interview he added, 'I think my reputation is something I'll probably try to spend the rest of my life living down. I have got a temper but I'm 100 per cent reliable on the set.'

It's clear that he's still bitter about the hotel incident, remarking to the US chat show *60 minutes*: 'Where I come from, a confrontation like that, as basic and simple as that, would have been satisfied with a handshake and an apology ... Your [US] legal system is very open to be misused.'

A host of directors and actors who have worked with Russell have defended him – often starting off with 'He's difficult but...' – but if there is anyone who knows Russell better than most on a working level, it's Ridley Scott. 'Really, what it is, is that Russell is very smart and therefore asks all sorts of intelligent questions, so if you're not ready you're going to get caught in the crossfire. So you'd better be ready. 'I'm used to him now. He's fundamentally a bit of a puppy dog.'

In a more candid moment, Russell has revealed that his anger issues stem from low self-esteem. 'I think I've got better over the years with just being OK with all that. Any negativity I had with it stems from self-worth issues. I don't rate myself or consider myself to be worthy of that sort of thing. So when people approach me my reaction is sometimes negative. But I'm a lot calmer with it now.

'[The public] don't see the crusty reality. They see some sort of sparkling version, and that's what they want to have contact with. I'm a lot easier about all that sort of stuff now.'

That Crowe should play a journalist in *State of Play* is somewhat ironic, given his past feisty experiences with the media and the paparazzi in general. 'Our privacy laws are non-existent. The one sentence that's in [the legislation] is "what a reasonable society expects". And a reasonable society could not possibly expect you to doorstop someone seven days a week, 24 hours a day, sit outside their house, follow them wherever they go – that's stalking.

'If it was happening to anyone else the police would have powers to do something about it. This bullshit excuse that they're just doing their job. It gets dangerous, too.'

Journalist Terry Amour recounted in his 2003 *Chicago Tribune* article that after accompanying Russell to a White Sox baseball game, he sighed to him, 'What you're going to see in a magazine somewhere soon is a photograph of us walking in here. It will say, 'Russell Crowe and bodyguards'. Whenever I go out with a group of my friends, it's always written up as being FBI, bodyguards or some [crap] like that.

'The paparazzi – they're sort of like parasites. It's amazing sometimes. We get followed everywhere. They stalk you, they set you up and all that sort of stuff. But if you get too upset about it, it's going to drive you crazy your whole life. I guess you can get pissed off about it as a bloke, but then again, you can get pissed off about anything. You're driving along the street and someone cuts you off. You get pissed off for a second and then life continues.'

RB Brenner, the journalism adviser on *Body of Lies*, was warned by Macdonald that Russell 'doesn't necessarily see the noble side of my profession' before they began working together. But Brenner was impressed with the 'articulate ally' that he could see now.

There seems to be a contradictory side to Russell. While he's made no secret of his distaste for the media, he's also gone out of his way to make sure journalists were on his side with a gruff charm offensive. In 2009, the *Sydney Telegraph* published an article mocking his fitness regime after he was spotted smoking a cigarette and eating fast food during a bike ride. Annoyed at the cartoon that accompanied the article by gossip columnist Annette Sharp, he challenged her to a 12-mile cycle ride through Sydney.

Not that everyone is sympathetic with Russell about the negative press. His *L.A. Confidential* co-star and fellow Antipodean, Guy Pearce, said, 'I admire Russell's talent, and am envious of it. But I don't admire the attention he gets. Although I think he brings some of that shit upon himself.'

Despite gaining a grudging respect for journalists after playing one in *State of Play*, Russell's true feelings about reporters would still find a way to surface. 'Only at fleeting moments did he offer hints of his own feelings about journalists,' Brenner recalled. One such occasion was when he was asked by Mirren, playing his executive editor, whether he could be objective on a particular story. Crowe, in character, veered off script. 'Absolutely not,' he said.

'Those words didn't make it into the film, much to my relief!'

CHAPTER TWENTY-FOUR

OTHER SIDES TO CROWE

'I don't need anybody else to pat me on the back and say, "You know what? You are a real musician." Stick your "real" in your ass, mate. I've been doing it all my life.'

– Russell Crowe

Russell's former band mate Graham Silcock remembers an encounter with Tom Sharplin not so long ago. 'He came into the shop the other day and mentioned that Russell said he'd like to do a Santana feel for a song. Tom apparently said, "You want someone who plays like Santana?" Russell said, "No, we'll get Carlos Santana." He was serious about it. Now that he's got the power and the contacts, I guess he can do what he always dreamed of.'

There is a touch of sadness about Russell's affair with music. He loved playing with his band before they split – and if he could just tour on a whim at bars around the world he would, but it wouldn't be fair on his bandmates. However, while his talents lie in acting not music, if he had the choice he would prefer to be blessed with musical talent.

'From my early twenties and first professional musical, when there was some acting stuff required, I realised I was good at it. I am a virtuoso in my job in that there's not an actor I can't go into a scene with and be absolutely confident that, whatever is required of my character, I can do it. If it had been that way with my music, I would have never gone near acting. But I am a mediocre guitarist and have a so-so singing voice. If I could sit with Eric Clapton, play guitar and get him to give me a little wink, that would be perfect. I know it is not going to happen, because the talent is not there.'

He added, 'I'm the least ambitious person in the band when it comes to the band being in the people's eye. For me, it's just all about writing the songs and recording them the way I want them to be and the way that showcases the talents that are in the band. That for me is success. I don't need anybody else to pat me on the back and say "You know what? You are a real musician." Stick your "real" in your ass, mate. I've been doing it all my life and I'm gonna keep doing it. If you're annoyed by it now, gee whiz, you're gonna be really pissed in 10 years. So you might as well just relax.'

In 2001 Russell commented on the record industry, saying, 'We spoke to some of the biggest record companies in the world. It became obvious they didn't give a shit about what we were doing. I guess I can understand that. They're there to sell records, and that would mean cashing in on the singer's Hollywood celebrity, and riding on the coat tails of the hit movies.

'We almost signed a deal with one label, and then I said, "Oh by the way, you can't release it for another six months." They freaked. They couldn't see the sense of not releasing it near one of my new movies. As far as I'm concerned – and I realise I'm in a privileged position where I can make these stands – if the record is going to sell, it should do it on its own merit. Listen, music is such a passion for me. I don't want anyone to prostitute it for me. If I wanted to be a slut, I'd do it myself.'

He had been with his band, 30 Odd Foot of Grunts, for 13 years but, even after a name change to The Ordinary Fear of God, he decided to forge his career as a solo artist. He played his first solo outing on 20 July, 2005 at a trendy Sydney club.

He had already suffered disappointment after his debut song *Raewyn* failed to chart in the Top 100 in either the UK or America. It was, he said, a song that made 'both men and women cry, think and call their parents.'

'I have emails from Sting and Billy Bragg, two of my writing heroes, that give testament to the quiet power of the song.'

However, Sting is said to have emailed Russell the following message – which proved to be wholly accurate: 'Your song is a royal gift to Charlie [Crowe's son] and

I'm touched you would send it to me. Will it get on the radio? Not a chance, mate. The days of the confessional, biographical song are over and not even you, Mr Crowe, can bring it back.'

It didn't help that his former bass player Garth Adams hit out at how the band had been disbanded. 'He didn't tell us he was going to do it. You'd think after all that time he would let us know personally, but no. I read about it in the newspapers.

'Once before he cancelled a tour and I heard about it on the radio. It's very disappointing but that's just the way he works.'

Apart from music, Russell loves his sports. He's a Leeds United fan but his real passion is rugby, as exemplified by his wearing a rugby shirt everywhere. He is known to sit down with some beers and a Chinese takeaway to watch re-runs of his favourite team, the South Sydney Rabbitohs. 'I was five when I first saw them,' he said. 'My dad took me along with a mate of his and the first match was Souths versus Saint George. We lost. Dad was a cheap bastard and got these tickets on the Hill, which was the rough section of the ground. I remember a point in the game where a decision went against us and the beer cans started flying and I was thinking, "What are we doing here?" But I was hooked.'

In 2003 he ran up a £1,000 phone bill following New Zealand in the World Cup, and he even paid $42,000 for the timekeeper's bell used for the team's first match in 1908.

In 2006, Russell and businessman Peter Holmes bought a 75 per cent share of the South Sydney club, when a £2.1 million bid was accepted by the shareholders – which saw Russell tell them: 'Let's vote yes. Let's get into bed together. I hope you respect me in the morning.'

After the bid was accepted he told journalists, 'People talk about the club being owned by the people because it serves a certain purpose, but I don't think a team that consistently runs last serves the community any purpose at all.'

Pledging to not take any profits, Russell insists that all money will be plowed back into the club. So what's it like owning a club you supported as a boy?

'It's incredible. But it's quite a tiring experience too. People say that we run it too emotionally, that we are too passionate about it. Is there such a thing? Can you be too passionate about the future of your players, their life during rugby, their life after rugby?'

Fans weren't won over easily, though, preferring the club be in the hands of the community rather than a Hollywood superstar. Russell has always had an association with the team, however. A year earlier he had visited the team's dressing room at half-time during a game when they were 12-6 down to the Canberra Raiders. Although, he never said anything directly to the players, they did win the game 29-16 and he promptly had a beer with them after the game. Coach Shaun McRae said at the time, 'It'd be nice to have him with us every week. His presence was felt by everybody.'

Russell's presence was a regular occurrence at the time because the players' uniforms were emblazoned with adverts for his forthcoming movie *Cinderella Man*. Explaining why he decided to have a sponsorship deal with them, he said, 'The South Sydney Rabbitohs... are currently the second-worst team, but we've had three or four years of being the worst team so we're on the way up.

'I did a sponsorship deal with them ... so for eight weeks this year [2005] the South Sydney team get to run out on the field with *Cinderella Man* on their shirt. Hopefully they'll start doing a bit better.'

When results started picking up soon afterwards, Russell said, 'It was really nice to come down, see a good, solid win. It's the last time I get to see a game this year in Australia and it means that in the five weeks so far that they've had *Cinderella Man* on their jerseys, they've won four out of five.'

His reign as co-owner started off in style when the Rabbitohs beat their rivals the Roosters 18-6, much to the obvious delight of Russell, who rushed to the changing rooms to congratulate his jubilant players.

Russell had made his mark straight away, getting rid of female cheerleaders in favour of a drumming band. 'We feel they made a lot of people uncomfortable. We examined game day and wanted to contemporise and make the focus football. It makes women uncomfortable and it makes blokes who take their sons to the football also uncomfortable.'

It was a move that pleased his wife too. 'She likes the fact that game day entertainment will be multi-sex. She likes that aspect. We've talked to a lot of people and everyone sees it as being progressive. The whole idea of percussion will be exciting for the crowd.'

Russell is so keen to see his team do well, he makes sure he can still watch his them even when he's in another country filming. Talking to *The Sunday Telegraph* in 2008, he said, 'I get to see every game these days by using a product called Slingbox, which is available here in America. The picture quality isn't spectacular but no doubt that will improve over time. Like everybody else, I've got to fit it around work time, but with the Slingbox if we can get an internet signal we are on.

'Recently on a night shoot for the film *State of Play*, I got to watch most of a game because the local real estate agent in a suburb of Washington DC let me sit in his office in the early hours and plug in a computer. His was the only business on the street that had a strong enough internet signal. I didn't see all of the game because I was shooting, but luckily by game time the dialogue scenes were finished and the rest of the night was shots of me walking down the street, so I could watch between takes.'

His enthusiasm for his team rubbed off on his co-stars.

McAdams explained, 'He was on set that day saying to all of us: "You have to come and watch the game. We're going to have meat pies." Russell is obviously a big supporter of his team and rugby league in general. He gave us all shirts, hats and scarves. I even got a [Rabbitohs] Christmas ornament. I wasn't familiar with rugby league beforehand and I don't profess to be an expert now. But everything I do know about rugby league, I know from Russell Crowe.'

But being owned by major movie star doesn't guarantee anything. In the summer of 2008 Russell's team experienced a slump in performances as well as a number of off-field incidents, including players breaking the team's drinking ban rule. Russell also had to put up with reports that his ownership style was too flashy, with the new Armani-designed uniforms in particular coming in for criticism.

In his defence, Russell said, 'We tried a lot of new things last year. In some areas we got lucky and new structures have held well; in others we have had less success and we have sought to deconstruct and start again. Our ultimate aim, and it is a goal we share with our members, is to make Souths cost effective across the board. We want our administration to be lean and mean and efficient in how it brings in the money required to run the team, and we want to provide our players game-leading facilities, medical care and motivation.

'Last year probably seemed too flashy for some, but a

lot of the things reported that we "splashed out" on, we didn't pay for. Armani suits is one prominent one. Mr Armani has been a friend for many years. He graciously designed and constructed that uniform for us out of his own generosity and what's more, he kitted out our new players this year as well. Like every Souths supporter, he too is waiting on some good news.'

Russell was also criticised for being too soft on the team. His hard-man image took a dent after he was spotted hugging his players and telling them that he loved them during a TV documentary on Russell's team.

John Sattler, a Souths player of the 1960s, said, 'It's a lot of bullshit. Imagine me walking up to [teammate] John O'Neill and saying I loved him and giving him a hug. He'd run. We had coaches like Clive Churchill and Bernie Purcell. They never said they loved us even when we won four premierships.'

A year later Russell had to make a public apology after a fight between one his players, David Fa'alogo, and the coach Jason Taylor.

Russell's relationship with his business partner Holmes eventually reached breaking point in 2008, with Holmes leaving the team. When reports claimed that he had been dumped after a fiery board meeting, where he was said to have warned investors that the club might not survive following a AUS$4 million loss and the team coming last in the league, Russell was forced to release a statement.

'It is the sensible thing to do,' he said. 'The reports of

our demise have been greatly exaggerated. Today the board applauded Peter's achievements in lifting the club and collectively we thanked him for his gargantuan effort over the past two years.'

An ambitious venture with Australian-born actor Anthony LaPaglia, who is a shareholder in Sydney FC football team, could see Russell's South Sydney Rabbitohs plying their trade in a joint 25,000-seat stadium. The *Without A Trace* star said, 'He [Crowe] wants a stadium, I want a stadium and we think together there is a possibility we might be able to pull it off. I would say if we could get the right people in the room at the same time, it is something that could happen in two to three years.'

CHAPTER TWENTY-FIVE

FAMILY MAN

'I think it comes to us all at a certain point... You get your priorities in place. I think he's really enjoying being a dad.'

– Ridley Scott

Russell's parents have been married for over 40 years, but apart from one girl, long-term relationships always eluded the actor. It seems they have always been hard to maintain with Russell. Certainly, if one famous story was to be believed, it would seem that the ladies in his life were in a ménage à trois – them, him and his ego.

His old friend Mark Rimington said, 'He was going out with a gorgeous ballerina during the show, but when she turned up he'd ignore her. He treated women like they were there for adornment rather than to be paid attention to.'

That certainly seems to ring true, with stories that one of Russell's girlfriends was only noted for driving him to his gigs in her Volkswagen, while another girl who had a one-night stand with him was somewhat shocked to find a signed copy of Russell's album under her pillow and him gone. Famously, when Russell was having sex with a young actress on location for *Proof* he could be heard hollering 'Go Russ, go!' in his trailer.

His *Romper Stomper* director, Geoffrey Wright, added, 'Russell seeks the company of women who are accomplished and secure, which usually means they're more mature. What separates him from other Hollywood guys is that he's not chasing teenage girls who are easy to outwit and manipulate. That's not to say he doesn't enjoy a good flirt or a one-night stand, but generally he seeks equals.'

He found that in Danielle Spencer.

At first just friends, they began dating after their 1990 movie *The Crossing* had finished and her relationship with her boyfriend had ended. 'We were both quite busy and scattered a bit, but we wrote a few letters and would phone each other and when we were in Sydney we would meet up. Our romance was a very gradual thing and it only really became possible when I split up from my boyfriend. Suddenly I was available and suddenly Russell could look at me in a different way. I knew him so well before it got romantic that the things I liked about him were things other than his good looks or sex appeal. I'd gone beyond that stage.

'He had to go to Melbourne for a film soon after we got together but he would send me little gifts all the time. I remember we once walked past a shop selling miniature dolls' house furniture and I said something about how I loved all that sort of thing. Well, he obviously remembered because when he went to Melbourne he kept sending me little bits and pieces – a miniature grand piano would arrive one day, then something else.

'He'd send funny toys and quirky things like those sponges you put in the bath and they blow up into animals when they're wet. He'd send things that would make you laugh, but he was just as capable of sending a beautiful bunch of red roses. He really is a very romantic and thoughtful person. He really knows how to make a girl feel special.'

Danielle would regularly stay at Russell's apartment, even sometimes when he was away filming. 'He would cook for me – his speciality was a barbecue – and he'd surprise me by buying a whole lot of seafood and bringing it home to cook. I don't think many men are good at doing housework, but from what I remember he did his share. He was a bit messy but I think we both were!'

Danielle would visit him on film sets: Russell was desperate for her to come see him on *The Quick and the Dead*. He was lonely, but he was also keen for Danielle to sample the environment.

'People forget it can get lonely living on set on your own for several months, even though it might look fun and glamorous,' she said. 'I think it was really grounding and very comforting for Russell to have someone special there with him, someone to say, "Hi, how are you?" after a busy day shooting.

'I sometimes regret that. I possibly should have taken the opportunity to explore some career options over there and done some auditions.

'I always felt that he deserved it. I have never ever seen anyone work as hard as Russell in my life. He is the most driven, hard-working person I have come across. I never doubted for a minute he would get there and I never ever resented it because I felt he deserved it and that he was a great actor. In fact, I couldn't see how he wouldn't get there. I'm very proud of him – I think he has done an amazing job.'

The couple split up in 1995 after nearly five years together. It was around the time that Russell was starting to make inroads with his acting career in America. It seemed that his career had the potential to take off and he had his perfect woman, but Danielle wasn't ready to live in Los Angeles.

'It was about life direction,' she said. 'Things were starting to happen for him and I didn't want to be in L.A.'

A friend told *New Idea* magazine, 'Russell had been going out with Danielle for nearly five years. He adored and respected her. He came to me one day in turmoil. He wanted to marry Danielle yet he was desperate to break into Hollywood.'

Danielle would only say, 'I was too young for marriage. I wasn't in marriage or baby mode.'

Talking about working away from home constantly putting a strain on relationships, she said, 'It's a problem for anyone in the entertainment industry, myself included. Russell always wanted to have a relationship like his parents but he knew it would be hard to attain. His parents have had a very solid, ongoing companionship for years, but when you're separated all the time and you're thrown into weird situations it can be quite destructive to your relationship.'

'We tried to keep the relationship going, but never at any time did we have a break-up,' Russell said. 'It was profoundly sad, but at the same time I wasn't going to say to her, "You must wait for me." Yet there probably weren't more than a few weeks in the 14 years from the time I met her, when we didn't communicate. There's a certain magical thing about me and her together.'

He added, 'I invited her to be my date for the Academy Awards, and when they announced that I had won I turned to her, and I leant down and said, "This is because you're here." And I gave her a kiss. It was just after that that we started seeing each other again as boyfriend and girlfriend.'

In another interview he said, 'It was more like a deep mutual respect, a mutual understanding. I have many, many things I'd like to say about Danielle. I've been thinking about it for a long time, I've known Dani for a long time.'

Danielle had seen Russell through it all – years of fruitless attempts to break into Hollywood, his highly publicised relationship with Meg Ryan and the Oscar wins. When they got back together it was clear to his family and friends that this time it was for good.

For Russell, it has always been Danielle. When he met her for the first time in 1989 for *The Crossing*, he was immediately smitten. 'I just really liked her. She had a stillness and a grace, which wasn't very usual in women her age – she was only 18 or 19 at the time. I just wanted to find out what was really going on behind those eyes.'

After their first meeting he would write the song 'Inside Her Eyes' – which would end up as his band's 2003 record.

His grand plans of courtship didn't always go to plan, however. One attempt saw him hiring a boat for her – unfortunately the only one he could get with a kitchen was one that seated 150 people.

'So this thing arrived and I thought, "Oh my God." It was just massive. I had all this fresh scampi and I was in the kitchen but it was almost a three-minute walk to get from the galley to where she was sitting on the deck. It could be a comedy in itself. She thought it was way over the top.'

Marriage is important to Russell. 'With the two of us at our ages, we both owed our parents a public marriage. My mum has been hoping for it since I was 16.

'I have my parents' marriage as a template. They've been married 45 years now and that's probably why I waited as long as I did – because I absolutely wanted to make sure that I only did it once.'

Both Russell and Danielle share a fondness for plain talking and don't suffer fools gladly. Recalling an incident when his wife was pregnant, Russell said, 'My wife is very straightforward. The other day she was being hassled by people saying she should go to classes. She said, "I know how to fucking breathe." Now you know why I married the girl.'

Danielle's big dream was a Roman wedding ceremony but Russell wasn't sure of the logistics involved flying to Italy. So he built a Byzantine chapel on his Australian estate instead. 'I needed to convince Danielle she didn't have to travel to Rome to get married like she'd always dreamed of, because I saw all the paperwork involved. I built her a Byzantine chapel of her own. It is consecrated and everything. In the long term, it really isn't extravagant at all, because we don't have to travel to Rome to see where we got married.'

Russell abstained from sex for three months before he married. 'We saw each other and stuff like that, but we didn't spend the nights together – just so the wedding night and the honeymoon and all that felt sort of new.'

They finally got married on 7 April, 2003, with Russell wearing a suit designed by his friend Giorgio Armani.

When Danielle announced that she was pregnant, Russell was delighted. He had carved a proper life for himself. He had a wife, a kid on the way and his parents and his brother all lived within an acre on his New South Wales farm.

'I didn't live in a house until I was 14,' he said. 'My dad changed employment once every 12 months, and that usually meant a change of apartments or hotels. Now I look at people who grew up in one house, one bedroom, and I'm jealous. Do I still yearn for that? Yeah, and what I've done with the farm is constructed around that. The place is big enough so that Mum and Dad and Terry – and me, when I'm there – can all live in it without being in each other's pockets. And I can pamper myself there, I can rest up, or I can do physical work. Or I can wander off into the bush and have absolute serenity.'

His farm holds a special significance for Russell. Backpacks are dotted around the buildings, filled with powdered milk, coffee, sugar and a metal cup so he can pick one up whenever he likes and go out and hike all day.

He said in 1997, 'If I ever feel I'm in danger of losing my perspective about the business of acting, I can always go home to the farm. My parents and older brother live there and they run the place when I'm away. I've set everything up at the farm so things should flow just fine when I'm away, and I try to be there when all the babies are being born – we have horses, cows, dogs and chickens.

'I'm just a big softie when it comes to the farm. These animals are my friends, and I enjoy spending time with them because they open my mind up again when the small world of show business threatens to close it down.' Talking about when his son Charlie was born, he admitted he had concerns. 'Yeah, I'm going to be there, absolutely. But I'm only allowed to look in certain areas. She wants me to focus on her and that's fine and dandy.

'Some people have got advice, some people have got horror stories. I like the people that just look you in the eye with that kind of glow and say, "It's all gonna be cool."'

His co-star Paul Bettany told him, 'I've told Russell to get as much sleep as possible stored up before it's born and to insist on sleeping time scheduled into all his shoots in the first 18 months.

'I'm also coaching him in the art of speed-eating. If you eat quickly, you can get a sneaky power nap in during the lunch break.'

Russell had picked up some parenthood tips during the filming of on *Master and Commander*, after stepping in to take care of 14-year-old Jack Randall when his mother had had to go back to England because of a family emergency. 'They were about to hire a professional chaperone and it came to my attention and I didn't want that energy on set. All the cast had family members and there were no outsiders, and I just thought the bringing in a professional chaperone might adjust the rhythm.

'So we got the paperwork done and he became my ward, and he stayed in the same apartment building that I stayed in and I took him to work every day and we had dinner together every night.'

He added, 'He's a very intelligent young boy but had never read a book, which I found to be just unbelievable. I was like, "I'm very sorry, mate – you're reading now. Here's your book and you've got three days to read it!"

'Jack was very much into reptiles, so I introduced him to [crocodile hunter] Steve Irwin. Irwin offered Jack a summer apprenticeship at the Australia Zoo.'

Charles Spencer Crowe was born on 21 December, 2003 at the Royal North Shore Hospital in Australia, weighing six pounds and two ounces. Russell was there to capture it all on film.

'I've got all the footage, and Dani actually said to me the next day, "You were fucking outrageous." Whenever I sense that she's getting a little uncomfortable, my focus is on her, but I make sure I put the camera somewhere where it still gets a good two-shot. And I don't stop or anything – one minute I'm shooting her, and you can see a little flicker of eyelid, of pain, or whatever. I'm seeing her, seeing the pain the angle going to her, checking she's OK and then I'm back into it.

'I've got cutaways. Anything interesting that's in the corridor, I've got a cutaway, too. I've got the feet of the nurse. She was wearing purple shoes. I've got lefts and rights, covered over shoulders both ways, just in case, because I didn't know how I'd want to do it.

'But, see, it was probably easier for me to deal with this huge thing that was happening by having this little thing to do, which was keep the video camera going.'

Talking about their decision to name their first child Charlie, Russell said, 'It was one of those odd things. When Dani wanted to call the baby Charlie, I said, "I don't think that'll go down very well in my family." We've had two Charles Crowes. One died scuba diving at 17. The other, the uncle of my grandfather, died in the Battle of Britain at 21. But Dani had had an Uncle Charlie who moved from

York to Hollywood and lived till he was 96. So I went on two things: a combination of genes and third-time lucky.'

Talking about Russell's parenting skills, his father-in-law, Don Spencer said, 'I think he'll be a fantastic dad. He's over the moon. We kept saying, "Has anyone else got a chance of holding this baby, Russell?" He said, "I'm bonding, I'm bonding!"'

Russell and Danielle welcomed their second child in the early hours of 7 July, 2006. He weighed eight pounds, and they named him Tennyson Spencer Crowe.

'We'll call him Tenny for short. My brother's name is Terry so that makes his initials TC as well, so slightly after him. But mainly because it's just different,' Russell said, shortly after the birth. 'Everybody is fine. The family is over there giving her big kisses and stuff. I am just going home to pick up Charlie to take him over to meet his new baby. We have been building him up pretty well for it. We have actually called it his baby.'

Russell has also talked about having more, kids, saying, 'I kind of get to this point where I'm spending most of my time telling stories about my kids ... It is the most special and wonderful thing. I'm continuously asking my wife about the possibility of expanding the brood.'

'I'd have a tribe if it was up to me. I just love being a dad. I love the privilege of having these extremely wonderful personalities in my life.'

The children are to receive a moving gift in 2032, where they can open a time capsule that Russell has buried. In it is a letter from him that says, 'Our lives have been blessed by you. Whatever comes along I will always love you with my whole being and soul. I know I would have brought you up to love your mother above all. My hope is that you find the things, people and love that bring you love and joy. Every day my life is better because I am a father.'

His loving family is now Russell's priority, and he admits that he finds it harder to justify his working schedule. 'The thing is with the jobs I am choosing these days is that they don't come with 26- or 38-week shooting schedules like some of the films I've done in the last few years.

'Every decision that I make now depends on what's right for my wife Danielle and my two young boys. Now that I'm getting a little bit older the bones are creaking and the Achilles tendons don't work the way they should. I don't approach everything with the same intensity that I used to.'

Russell was filming in New York when his wife phoned him. 'She was saying she heard all this noise in the corridor, so she went to check out what it was, and there's my son dragging a laden suitcase down the corridor.

'She said, "What are you doing?" He said, "I'm going to America to see Daddy." So they turned it into a game. Every day, he packs his bag now.

'How I keep them grounded is a good question and it's something I'm going to be dealing with for the rest of my life. That's the big gig, being a dad.'

CHAPTER TWENTY-SIX

RUSSELL CROWE AND HIS MERRY MEN

'I won't be playing two roles in Nottingham. If I ever were to do that, I'd pick roles that were more diverse, say Tuck and Marion.'

– Russell Crowe

With *Robin Hood* set for release in 2010, Russell was once again embarking on a project with Ridley Scott. 'It's just come about naturally,' he said. 'We probably should have worked together again straight after *Gladiator* because we each knew then that we really enjoyed each other's company and we enjoyed the way each other works.

'But I suppose it's not a usual thing and he went off and did his stuff and I went off and did mine. But after that cycle when he did those movies without me around, we just sat down one day and talked, and we both came to the conclusion that we liked being on set with each other, you know? I don't want to disparage anybody else I've ever worked with, but I just really like the way he makes a film.

'He has a great respect for the medium and how much it costs. He takes a very working-class attitude towards it and I appreciate that and I enjoy it too. I like to get to work and know we are going to achieve something every day.'

Russell originally signed on to play the Sheriff of Nottingham. The role, traditionally that of Robin Hood's arch-enemy, was to be given a new twist that saw the Sherriff portrayed in a more positive light as he investigates a murder. Robin Hood was to be more of a fallen hero in this version of the familiar tale.

'Part of the strength of the script was the simple idea of doing *Robin Hood* by making the Sheriff the good guy,' said Ethan Reiff, who was to work on the script.

Speaking before shooting began, Scott told *Empire*: 'I've already taken a walk in the woods and scouted out some locations. We've got Russell Crowe lined up to play the lead – he can do a really good English accent.'

Talking about the venture, Russell said, 'The world doesn't need a mundane version of *Robin Hood*. If we're gonna do it, we've got to kick some serious butt. When the idea came up and they gave me this script, I said, "Look, I don't like this. This doesn't work. It's not good enough." So this has got to be the best one ever done, otherwise I should be doing something else.

'I'm a big Robin Hood fan and have been since I was a little kid. We'll have a look at the Hollywood mythology and how much of that is embedded in the psyche of people when they think of Robin Hood. I'll tell you this – Richard the Lionheart won't be bounding up in the last scene and saving the day. Richard was a bloke who only spoke French. And who only spent six months of his 10-year reign in England.'

At one point the movie's title of *Nottingham* was axed. Russell said at the time, 'I think it's just going to be *Robin Hood*. There were lots of other ways of calling it and some different ideas. Prior to Christmas, the studio were talking about *Nottingham* as a title being well-known now, having been discussed for 18 months at the highest levels of press and marketing and stuff like that and it was a good – what they called a solid gold – name.

'And the question came up: "But is it better than *Robin Hood*?" And everybody just shook their head and said, "No, it's not."'

Despite the legend of Robin Hood having been translated onto the big and small screen numerous times, the film's producer Brian Grazer was convinced that the time was right for a reinvention.

'Oddly, it's a metaphor for today,' Grazer says. 'He's trying to create equality in a world where there are a lot of injustices. He's a crusader for the people, trying to reclaim some of the ill-gotten gains of the wealthy. That's a universal theme.'

Talking about Crowe's look in *Robin Hood*, he said, 'He doesn't have the old Robin Hood tights. He's got armour. He's very medieval. He looks, if anything, more like he did in *Gladiator* than anything we're used to seeing with Robin Hood.'

In another interview, he added, 'For every Robin Hood that has been made, there has never been a Robin Hood that could *be*. Everyone falls into the trap of, "Well, if you're doing Robin Hood you have to do this or that..."

'No, you don't have to hit the same notes you can take the time period, you can take the core message and put a different take on it.

Russell had decided to grow his hair for the part, but with work on *Body of Lies* and then *State of Play* under way, he had do it while working on the two films. Eventually, however, he decided to cut it because it was like 'walking around with a dead koala on your back'.

'I just got sick of it,' he added. 'I made two movies working around the length of the hair – just for *Robin Hood* – and then, once we finally got the green light and I knew that I had to click into the work-outs seriously, it didn't suit any more.'

Russell had to shed almost 50lb (23 kilos) for the part, using a gruelling exercise regime that saw him work out for three hours each day.

His Merry Men – Allan Doyle and Kevin Durand who play Allan A'Dale and Little John – visited Russell's farm to exercise and bond. Scott Grimes, who plays Will Scarlett couldn't make it because of scheduling difficulties on his TV show *ER*.

And bond they did; they would work out, jog, go bike riding and practise archery – a sport that Russell loved.

'And then at night a lot of music, because that's an important part of the story," revealed Doyle.

Doyle apart, it was reunion of sorts for the Merry Men – both Grimes and Durand worked with Russell on *Mystery, Alaska.*

Talking to *Empire*, Russell insisted that this sort of bonding was important to the story.

'What you get is a group of people completely connected to the movie that they are doing. The bonding that works for a sports team in real life is the same and is essential for a group of actors. I know these guys and I trust them and we have that connection, it's a given.

'You bring together people with a common cause and you work towards a certain level of personal effort and an ambition of excellence. Who knows if you get there, right? The variables are huge, but if you don't start out trying to get that then you're never going to get even close.'

He would also learn archery – something Russell threw himself into.

'Man, I loved it. It's great. I said to the guy who was teaching me, "I'm in love with the flight. I just love it when the arrow is released from the bow." And he was like, "Well, it's your sport then."'

Working with Cate Blanchett was a thrill for Russell. 'So far we have ridden horses together, seen off bad guys, got naked (partially), wallowed chin deep in mud, danced by firelight, attended a funeral and kissed. What can I say? It's an interesting gig. I can't talk highly enough of her skill and sense of humour. She is a wonderful partner in crime and now that we are under way, I can't think of anyone else in this part.'

That comment wouldn't have pleased Sienna Miller, who was originally attached to the part before being replaced by Blanchett. Speaking about her disappointment, she said generously, 'If I had to make a choice between myself and Cate, then I'd choose her as well. Of course I was disappointed, but I am also big enough to know these things happen all the time in the film industry – it's just that when they happen to me it's news.'

Russell would later say, 'I appreciate Cate's artistry a lot but Sienna would have been wonderful in the role anyway.'

For Russell and Scott it was a chance to work in Surrey again, in the same English landscape that they had worked while shooting scenes for *Gladiator*.

'It was crazy being back there,' Russell said. 'From the moment we turned into Fareham, it was like, "Yeah, here it is, this place where the big part of my public life began." *L.A. Confidential* was great and it got me into sleazy nightclubs for free, but it didn't really change my life. *Gladiator* changed my life completely.

'On set, all day, people were asking, "What happened there?" and I was like "Well, that's Marcus Aurelius' tent, that's where the encampment with the hospital was, that was Maximus' tent, this is the archery line, that's where I saw the bird..." It all came back to me, and they are great memories.'

When any great British tradition gets the Hollywood treatment, the domestic press take a keen interest – and always not in a good way. *Robin Hood* was no exception. Once filming had started, it seemed that something bad happening on set was an almost daily occurrence.

One such story suggested that Russell was banned from a Surrey pub because of his unruly behaviour – a ban, according to the landlord, that was repeated by other establishments nearby. Crowe's manager, Grant Vanderberg, said, 'The only truth to the whole thing is that he has been [to the pub]. He has been there four or five times with his kids. There is a playground in the back.'

Then thousands of pounds worth of camera equipment was also stolen when five hooded burglars made off with it. A crew member suffered neck injuries after he fell into a pit at Shepperton studios, and an actor was injured during a battle scene.

Some could be dismissed as fodder for a slow news day, but talks of a long-running feud between Russell and Scott during the production of *Robin Hood* were more surprising, especially considering their working history together.

After New York gossip column Page Six reported that studio bosses had had to fly to set to placate the pair, Russell was quick to explain their 'passionate' relationship. 'Ridley and I have never made a secret of the way we work. We agree to disagree because in the calculation of both our opinions we create the best idea. There's no yelling, no diva bullshit – we are doing our jobs to the best of our abilities and try to do something special every day.'

Universal's chairman Marc Shmuger explained, 'Ridley and Russell asked us to visit to see more than an hour of footage they've already shot, which was nothing short of spectacular. Russell and Ridley are working on their fifth film together and have one of the strongest and most collaborative working relationships. When it's news that a studio chairman and a film's producer [Brian Grazer] visit a production, it must be a very slow gossip day.'

Perhaps in a bid to distance himself from the deluge of bad press, stories of Russell's generosity started to spring up. It was hardly subtle – stories of Russell donating thousands of pounds worth of goods to a charity shop, tipping bar staff £600 and even buying a crew member a car were reported to the press.

Denise Yarde, a boom mic operator on the film, was bought the car after her vehicle went up in flames on her way to work. She got annoyed at Crowe's constant need to make light of the situation, and snapped, 'Well, I suppose it's OK for you Russell. You've probably never had to worry about finding £5,000 for a car.' Hours later, she was stunned to find Russell handing her a large amount of cash, saying, 'There you go. You can buy a £10,000 car now.'

He also arranged for a £60,000 battering ram prop used in the movie to be given to a Scottish battle re-enactment group.

Charlie Allan, the chief executive for the Clanranald Trust, had played a German warrior in Gladiator, and he and Russell have been friends ever since. He said, 'When Russell asked me if I had approached production to ask for props from the set to take to our project, I said I hadn't and Russell suggested I speak to Charles Schlissler, the executive producer.

'So next morning we were standing on set waiting to get going and Russell arrived with a huge grin on his face, and tugging in an excited manner at my sleeve, asked me to come over with him to look at something. We stood at the top of the hill and he said "See that battering ram?"

'Right there and then the penny dropped and I looked at him in disbelief and said, "You're shittin' me, man?" and he laughed and said, "It's yours."

Allan said about making the movie, 'The atmosphere on *Robin Hood* was much different from *Gladiator*. The scenes and the rapidity of the pace of filming were amazing. There were lots of cameras and angles were being shot from several directions at once. There was a fun atmosphere too, serious but still fun. Two night shots in a row were delayed for a short time while Russell and the Merry Men gathered us all in and gave some eye-opening performances to the extras. The camera crews were clock watching but Russell was making sure everyone was happy and in good spirit. He is a great singer and has some great lyrics.'

Robin Hood is not only a first for Russell in terms of playing one of his childhood heroes, but he is one the film's producers – a new role that has left him drained. Talking to *Entertainment Tonight*, he said, 'Being a producer has changed the experience for me – it's a lot more stressful. It's natural for me to worry about things anyway, because I care about it, but now I have to officially care about things, even if I don't care.

'It's been two years, it's been a long haul – it actually should be one of those things where it's the most fun job I've done for years but it isn't. There's a lot of stress involved, now that I'm learning, so I'm empathising more with the people I've worked with for years, like Ridley.'

Talking about the film, he said, '*Robin Hood* is a huge part of English-speaking people's history, possibly the oldest living story in the English language. It's a big job to reshape that in people's minds, particularly when you have 100 years of cinema on top of all the books that came before that, but we're giving it a go.'

He added, 'The comparison between *Robin Hood* and *Gladiator* is no bad thing at all. We've done some things in this where we knowingly go into that territory. As

Ridley has said, if you're going to doff your cap to an influence, it's OK if it's your own. It's been ten years. Other people have tried to do it and not come anywhere near, so I don't have a problem doffing that cap.'

Like *Robin Hood*, Russell's future films will always be interesting.

In an interview during filming of *Gladiator*, he remarked, 'I wanted to work with the best actors I possibly could. I wanted to do the greatest work I possibly could. And I can do that because I've kept focused. I've done what I set out to achieve.'

It's a business model of sorts that he adhered to all so long ago, and it's one that he has kept up since then and one you assume he will for a long time to come.

But for someone who has such a colourful personal life, it's fitting that his roles show more of the man than the tabloid headlines: the aggressive machismo of Maximus, the barely restrained anger of Jeffrey Wigand, the driven, never-say-die spirit of Jim Braddock. As Russell says, 'If you want to know me, watch my movies'.